.... ❦ ....

PRAISE FOR *UNDER THE DOME*

"Jean Daive's memoir of his brief but intense spell as confidant and poetic confrère of Paul Celan offers us unique access to the mind and personality of one of the great poets of the dark twentieth century."

—J.M. COETZEE, Recipient, Nobel Prize in Literature

"An intimate portrait in fragments? An utterly singular memoir? An essay in poetics? A poem in prose? All these and more. This fluid and indefinable work by Jean Daive has never been far from my thoughts since I first read it decades ago. It breathes with Celan while walking with Celan, walking in the dark and the light with Celan, invoking the stillness, the silence, of the *breathturn* while speaking for the deeply human necessity of poetry. Now, we are fortunate once again to have available Rosmarie Waldrop's pitch-perfect translation in this most welcome new edition."

—MICHAEL PALMER, author of *The Laughter of the Sphinx*

"'The world always remembers poetry,' says Celan in this staggering epic of talking and silence and walking and translating at tables. It is his poetry that is indeed remembered, however we in the world come to it. The fragments textured together in this more-than-magnificent rendering of Jean Daive's prose poem by this master of the word, Rosmarie Waldrop, grab on and leave us haunted and speechless."

—MARY ANN CAWS, author of *Creative Gatherings: Meeting Places of Modernism* and editor of the *Yale Anthology of Twentieth Century French Poetry*

"Written in the rhythm of walking, and in the very particular rhythm of walking beside Paul Celan, this stunning book-length prose-poem honors not only the great Romanian-born poet but also the life-long love affair with the word that poetry requires. One of the most important poets of post-WWII France, Daive alone has the consummate sensitivity and mastery of nuance needed to make Celan present again and to evoke the rich background of time and place that allows the story to attain its proper historic proportions. Rosmarie Waldrop's brilliant translation resonates with her profound knowledge of both Celan's and Daive's poetry and the passion for language that she shares with them. The text brings these three major poets together in a highly unusual and wholly successful collaboration."

—COLE SWENSEN, author of *On Walking On*

"'We never talk about Paul Celan,' certainly not as is done in *Under the Dome*. In this gem of a poetic memoir, we are as close to breathing and metabolizing the stubborn silences of Paul Celan as it is possible to do so while honoring his life and art. 'Would you translate me?' becomes the code and kernel from which the infinity of Paul Celan's tragic genius unfolds. How else to talk, sing, or communicate with Paul Celan—who died trying to unpave the road on which the ineffable treads—if not through unraveling language? If Paul Celan's life force is genomic, or elemental, it replicates and transfers itself through us like a Spinozan miracle. Rosmarie Waldrop takes up Celan's question to Jean Daive as her own. I cannot unread her inimitable ease in these pages. This is a book that contends with time."

—FADY JOUDAH, author of *Footnotes in the Order of Disappearance*

"The republication of this arresting translation of Jean Daive's writing about his conversations and encounters with Paul Celan lets us imagine the space and time of Celan's words as they were uttered on the streets of Paris, in its cafés, under the trees, and by the river. Daive's writing is a highly punctuated recollection, a memoir, perhaps a testimony, but also surely a way of attending to the time of the writing, the conditions and coordinates of Celan's various enunciations, his linguistic humility. Yet the words sometimes break free of any context, lingering in a separate space on the page; they follow lived memory, the well-worn interruptions whose repetition finds no resolution. Daive offers small stories, but mainly fragments that follow one another in the wake of the destruction of narrative flow; the tenses change suddenly, putting into a shifting modality of writing a complex memory that refuses to leave a friend. Celan's death, what Daive calls 'really unforeseeable,' remains as an 'undercurrent' in the conversations recollected here, gathered up again, with an insistence and clarity of true mourning and acknowledgement."

—JUDITH BUTLER, author of *The Force of Nonviolence*

Under the Dome

Jean Daive

Under the Dome

walks with Paul Celan

translated by Rosmarie Waldrop

City Lights Books

Originally published by Editions P.O.L (Paris, France) as *La Condition d'infini 5: Sous la coupole* © 1996 by Jean Daive

English translation originally published as *Under the Dome: Walks with Paul Celan* (Burning Deck: Serie d'écriture No. 22)
Translation Copyright © 2009 by Rosmarie Waldrop

First City Lights Edition: 2020
Introduction Copyright © 2020 by Robert Kaufman and Philip Gerard

Cover photograph: "Paul Celan, 1967" © Renate von Mangoldt
Author photograph: "Jean Daive, 2020" © Garrett Caples

Library of Congress Cataloging-in-Publication Data

Names: Daive, Jean, author. | Waldrop, Rosmarie, translator.
Title: Under the dome : walks with Paul Celan / Jean Daive ; translated by Rosmarie Waldrop.
Other titles: Condition d'infini. 5, Sous la coupole. English
Description: San Francisco, CA : City Lights Books, 2020.
Identifiers: LCCN 2020022279 (print) | LCCN 2020022280 (ebook) | ISBN 9780872868083 (trade paperback) | ISBN 9780872868120 (epub)
Subjects: LCSH: Celan, Paul--Fiction.
Classification: LCC PQ2664.A46 C6613 2020 (print) | LCC PQ2664.A46 (ebook) | DDC 843/.914--dc23
LC record available at https://lccn.loc.gov/2020022279
LC ebook record available at https://lccn.loc.gov/2020022280

City Lights Books are published at the City Lights Bookstore,
261 Columbus Avenue, San Francisco, CA 94133
www.citylights.com

Contents

With Paul Celan

Robert Kaufman &
Philip Gerard

In this centenary year of his birth—lamentably also the fiftieth anniversary of his suicide—City Lights makes a special contribution to the ongoing international commemorations of Celan with a new edition of Jean Daive's *Under the Dome: Walks with Paul Celan*, luminously translated from the French by Rosmarie Waldrop. City Lights' re-publication of Daive's superb book, whose point of departure is the experience of two poets translating one another, stands as a kind of recursive poetic justice, for City Lights was the first press here in our Americas to issue a book of poetry featuring translations of Celan. Recounting the history that brought this poetry to Western-Hemisphere audiences allows us to appreciate how Daive's work likewise helped foster engagements with Celan's art that mattered—that continue to matter—on both sides of the Atlantic and beyond.

In Winter 1957–58, *The Hudson Review* published Jerome Rothenberg's translations of seven poems by the German-Jewish poet Erich Kästner, who had somehow survived the Third Reich while remaining in Germany throughout the Hitler period. Alongside his translations, *The Hudson Review* also published Rothenberg's commentary about the poems' dissident, biting, cabaret-satire form.[1] City Lights founder Lawrence Ferlinghetti, seeing the work in *The Hudson Review*, quickly proposed that Rothenberg edit a volume of contemporary German poetry for the press. *New Young German Poets*—translated, edited, and introduced by Rothenberg—appeared in 1959 as Pocket Poets Series Number Eleven. Shortly before the volume issued, Robert Bly's magazine *The Fifties* ran three selections from a larger set of Rothenberg translations: renderings into English of an astonishing German-language poet named Paul Celan, one of the "new young German poets" about to receive wider American attention via City Lights (though it should be observed that, at 39, Celan didn't deem himself young, nor had the Rumanian-born, now-French-citizen Celan ever been German). Among the 10 artists Rothenberg presented in *New Young German Poets* were the Austrian Ingeborg Bachmann; Günter Grass; Hans Magnus Enzensberger; and Celan, "regarded by many," Rothenberg noted, "as the greatest of the post-war poets in Germany, perhaps in Europe." Celan had the most poems in the volume, including "Corona," "Shibboleth," and of course, "Death Fugue" (which had appeared, as translated by the art critic Clement Greenberg, in the March 1955 issue of the then-still-progressive *Commentary*). Rothenberg's prefatory remarks to *New Young German Poets* stressed the importance of the poetry's emergence from fascism, the national-socialist genocide, and their Cold-War aftermaths.

In fact, these "new young" poets were not simply a next generation of German poetry; any such continuity had been broken by the war and genocide, even when the postwar "economic miracle" seemed to make the catastrophic past decades disappear. The poets Rothenberg selected had ambivalent relationships to the new West Germany, often living beyond its borders and feeling themselves, as Enzensberger wrote to Rothenberg, "fremde"—strangers, aliens, outsiders—within "the forlorn society of todays [sic] Western Germany, which lives in terms of consumption substituted for freedom, of power and defence hysteria, etc."[2]

New Young German Poets was well positioned to reach readers and makers of poetry in both direct and roundabout ways. Audiences (primarily in the U.S., but likewise in Canada, the Caribbean, Latin America) who made a habit of getting hold of and sharing City Lights books included poets associated with the Black Mountain, San Francisco Renaissance, and New York School groups, as well as those connected to the Objectivist project. The connections stretched further: by the early 1970s, for example, *Savacou: A Journal of the Caribbean Artists Movement* (founded and edited by the Barbadian poet Kamau Brathwaite and colleagues) published poet and theatre director Alex Gradussov's rendering of "Death Fugue" into an English that aimed to reach Antillean readers, in a special issue that honored one of the key figures of Caribbean writing and activism, Frank Collymore.[3] Meanwhile, in an overlapping time-signature, through the translations in Rothenberg's own new magazine *Poems from the Floating World*, as well as those published in *New Young German Poets*, Robert Duncan was introduced to Celan, an encounter that deepened through the years. By the mid- to late 1970s, that encounter had generated Duncan's "A Song from the Structures of Rime Ringing as the Poet Paul Celan Sings."[4]

Rothenberg's early work on *New Young German Poets* led him into a special trajectory at once generous and dedicated to genuine explorations of collective human experience in its diversity; he's often looked back on what he's called his ever-increasing understanding of the importance of meeting and talking with Celan when serving with the U.S. Army in West Germany in 1953–54. Rothenberg has always emphasized the significance, to any consequential poetics, of *translation*. This is to say that Rothenberg had imagined from the get-go a "globalism" that, far from imposing a worldwide standardizing equivalence onto all literary, aesthetic, and cultural objects, instead would seek "not an everywhere that was nowhere but an everywhere made up of many somewheres."[5]

* * *

Midway through the decade when *New Young German Poets* first circulates across the Americas—as the world itself convulses in what becomes known as "the '60s"—Celan, home in Paris, meets the young, unpublished French poet and translator of German-language poetry, Jean Daive. Celan asks Daive to translate some of his poetry; Daive agrees.

Composed about 20 years later and published in 1996—as the fifth volume in Daive's continuing series-project *La Condition d'infini (The Infinite Condition)*—*Sous la coupole* hauntingly traces in elliptical concentric circles the two poet-translators' working relationship and friendship that lasted from 1965 until Celan's April 20, 1970 suicide. In the mode or form of temporal recurrence and echo, musical theme and variation; in movements that seem never to have started from any single defined point of origin but that course like memory waves: we read and hear, once and again—yet differently, even when incidents and occasions might appear the same—of their innumerable work sessions, often a return in remembered-time to the same session. The echoes are not only of what's already come, in *Under the Dome*, but also of many of the Celan poems necessarily folded into the book's music-like memory-structure. Indeed, the connections between this iterative movement and translation itself are enacted as, into, Daive's poetics. We read of work sessions that are followed by... walks and talks; coffees followed or preceded by... walks and talks; dinners that come after yet still precede more... walks and talks; and—sometimes, just simply—walks and talks. With silence a crucial component of what it means to walk, to talk, to put the two into relation. World and poetry too are distinct, with the *how?* of their mutual engagement an ever-present question. "His silence is an electric switch," Daive writes of Celan, a "commutateur," because it redirects the flow of current, translating speech, changing the direction (*sens*)—and the sense (*sens*)—of communication.

The "dome" of the book's title refers in the first place to the shade-shelter formed by the trees' foliage, the "foliage" that, in French and German, among other languages, yields terms that can signify "leaf" or "page": *feuille*; *Blatt*. The trees—primarily chestnut and paulownia—that populate the Place de la Contrescarpe in Paris' Fifth Arrondissement where Celan lives, and in whose streets and cafés Celan and Daive delight to stroll, to think aloud, to work: these trees and their leaves generate—and in turn offer the poet-translators a generative—dome. The leafy dome of the Contrescarpe becomes one of those particularized "somewheres" that together make up the collective yet differentiated "everywhere" Rothenberg refers to above. The Contrescarpe is somewhere for these two poets and their two-and-more languages to meet, but its dome is not a container. It is fitting that the *feuilles* and *Blätter* are now, via the inevitable Whitmanian pun, projecting their shadows in English. "The secret is in these leaves," Waldrop translates, echoing in a minor key the opening of *Leaves of Grass*: "Have you felt so proud to get at the meaning of poems?" Daive and Celan's walks are quite different from Whitman's loafing; the American poet's confidence that the pages of the poem might adequately gloss the leaves of the world has notably withered. And yet, Celan himself recognized how his own view that there is "no basic difference between a poem and a handshake" resonated with Whitman's assertion, "Camerado, this is no book,/who touches this touches a man"—a transatlantic solidarity that runs all the deeper for the spectral quality of these person-to-person contacts.

Another of those lines from *Leaves of Grass*: "Have you practis'd so long to learn to read?" Our experience, of reading—and reading the "reading-matter" of all kinds in the somewheres that make up everywhere—announces itself as our co-participation in *Under the Dome*'s initial moment when we read (in our first encounter with this book, and with Celan) about Celan *reading* in order to engage what's known—or not known, or not yet known—of the world:

> No matter whom, no matter what, Paul Celan
> reads no matter where because the word drives him
> to memory and is the imaginary space where the
> legibility of the world is acted out...

> The world is illegible and the matter of words
> engenders a structure: the poem. Vibration of
> sense used as energy...

He reads the newspapers, all of them... posters,
catalogues, dictionaries and philosophy...

He reads Rilke, Trakl, Kafka, Heidegger. Listens
to conversations, notes a word heard in a store, in
the street...

The matter of words. Words as matter...

* * *

Reading Daive or Celan could never be described as "a walk in the
park"—not for readers of French and German, and not even for
the two poets themselves, who read each other between such strolls.
English-reading audiences have had access, periodically, to parts of
Daive's oeuvre; a good deal more of it has appeared as the result of
a number of co-translations he and the Canadian-U.S. poet Norma
Cole have done of one another's work during the last decade.[6] Celan's
presence in English goes further back but the trials of his translators
have not ceased to be daunting.

So there's an almost perfect bookending—though happily, not
an ending—to what's constructed in 1959 by *New Young German
Poets*: that since at least the early 1990s, Rothenberg's collaborator
on the ongoing anthology series *Poems for the Millennium* has been
the French-born, Luxembourg-raised poet and translator Pierre
Joris, who's moved among Europe, North Africa, and the U.S. for
the better part of six decades, prolifically translating among French,
German, English, Arabic, and other languages. A crucial portion of
Joris' work has involved bringing more and more of Celan's poetry
and critical writing closer to the kind of English translations they
demand. No one's expressed the judgment better than Mary Ann
Caws: "Without simplifying, aiming at anything elegantly 'poetic,' or

is in question, the translatability of the world uncertain. *"Dé – porté"* is already one of these language fragments, a word that Daive splits in two and disposes like the linked wagons of a freight train. As the translation of the lines "Verbracht ins/Gelände"—which Pierre Joris renders as "Brought into/the terrain"⁹—Daive's *"Dé – porté dans l'étendue"* was subjected to fierce critique when it was first published in the Mercure de France in 1971 because of its violent treatment of the word "verbracht," a participle that usually denotes a passage of time and that commands the sense of "déporté" (*deported*) only in the reports of a bureaucrat.¹⁰ Technically, "verbracht" does not count among the many "Komposita" that Celan threads through his poetry, and yet Daive's translation reads it as such a composite, breaking it down and translating the fragments piecemeal: "ver-" (*dé-*), "-bracht" (*-porté*). Of course, parsing "ver-bracht" as "dé-porté" makes plain the history which Celan's poem leaves implicit: in French, "la déportation" refers explicitly to the German-operated network of freight trains that carried Jews like Celan's parents to their deaths in concentration camps. As Waldrop translates, "my parents died deported."

How, then, to translate Daive's *"Dé – porté"*? Certainly, the cognate "deported" or "de – ported" offers itself. Less historically specific than "déporté," "deported" expands the range of reference, opening the poem onto a longer, ongoing history of state violence. But it forgoes the gamble of Daive's direct invocation of the genocide, a roll of the "die" (*dé*) which risks losing the German so that it may name the vanished world with which that language is nonetheless freighted. Violently glossing the historical rupture by which the euphemistic, Eichmannian "verbracht" became, in effect, an other German—a lexeme in what Victor Klemperer called the *Lingua Tertii Imperii*—Daive's French bears witness to the loss of Celan's mother tongue, pointing to the unsayable difference that distinguishes the language he shared with his mother (verbracht) from the language in which her murder was commissioned (ver-bracht).

That the repetition of this loss is what is at stake in the translation is evident from Daive's recollection of the "violent stroke across

8

the paper" with which Celan sanctions Daive's solution. *Under the Dome* is full of such convulsive motions: lightning flashes, the gambler throws the dice, the engraver defaces the plate, and the poem, we learn, "crosses out the world." By courting destitution, however, all of these gestures refer us back to this paradoxical movement of (self-)translation, whereby Celan "authorizes" his poem's exile into French and thus becomes the "author" of his own linguistic dispossession. "Have you ever thought of writing in another language?... Yes, sometimes, in French... But it is not possible." What is not possible in writing, however, may be possible in translation. Contrary to received wisdom, translation can have a generative relationship to its alleged impossibility. Here, for instance, the impossibility of writing in French opens up the singular possibility of mourning the loss of German in the translation.

And in English? It tells us a lot about the layers of language and memory that make up *Under the Dome*'s vault that Waldrop declines to translate "*Dé – porté dans l'étendue*" as she translates the rest of Daive's French. Here, Daive does more than transmit the sense of "Verbracht ins/Gelände"; the violent dislocation of French morphology bears the trace of the crime—"das Verbrechen"—that echoes in the German. Waldrop, translating the French, is thus justified in leaving this language fragment "in the original," since this French is not only French. It is freighted with Celan's German, which, though deported into French, retains its "unmistakable trace."

"With the unmistakable trace" is the third verse of "Engführung." The fourth, "Grass written asunder," produces another unexpected echo of Whitman's master trope—this time turned inside out. Writing scatters the leaves. Its track winds through the mute spaces between. Such negative spaces are also suggested by the text's titular dome. In addition to naming the luminous canopy of the Contrescarpe, Daive's dome translates the "vault" of Celan's 1967 poem "Grosse glühende Wölbung" (*Vast, glowing vault*). The vault of that poem is no sheltering sky; indeed, the abyss opened up by receding constellations seems to

9

consume the shared world. In "Vast, glowing vault," a form of relation persists despite this withdrawal, manifesting itself as an unworldly obligation to the other. That poem's vision of an ethical relation that survives catastrophe helps explain why its final line, "Die Welt ist fort, ich muß dich tragen" (*The world is gone, I must carry you*), reverberates throughout Daive's recollection of his friend. An early variation on the theme appears in the text's original French edition as:

> Le verbe n'est plus.
> Le monde n'est plus (fort).
>
> Il faut que je te porte.

Lines which Waldrop translates as:

> The word is no more,
> The world is no more (no stronger).
>
> I have to carry you.

The withdrawal of the word and the world has obvious Biblical overtones. In this translated *memoire* of translation especially, the absence of "verbe" and "monde" also resonate plainly with Waldrop's task as a translator (the connection is not incidental: in Celan's Bible, we learn, the seventh day is set aside for translation).

Left behind in the movement from Celan's "Welt" to Daive's "monde" and then to Waldrop's "world," the word is not only literally absent; its absence seems to be compounding. The original's disappearance in the translation had already been recalled in Daive's "Le monde n'est plus (fort)," which appends the missing "fort" (gone) from "Die Welt ist fort" to the end of the French verse. Of course, Daive's "fort" does not restore Celan's word, though the mournful reminder might give French the strength to bear its absence.

Translation implies loss, always; the real question is, how does the translation carry its losses? Paradoxically, a translation grows stronger *as a translation* for coming to terms with what cannot be retrieved. Waldrop's translation does just this, conjuring the strength to carry the vanished world "under the dome" out of the eclipse of that strength and the loss of that world. Her translation reads in Daive's "(fort)" not just the German adjective predicating absence (fort) but the French adjective signifying strength (fort). The interlingual pun does not translate well in English, nor is non-translation a viable option as it had been with "*Dé – porté.*" "Fort" has its English meaning too, one which would draw energy from the electrical switch that toggles between Daive's "strong" and Celan's "gone." Additionally, Daive's line, although freighted with Celan's diction, remains fluent French, its parenthesis resolvable into correct French syntax. "Le monde n'est plus fort" (*The world is no longer strong.*) Waldrop's English, by contrast, possesses no such fluency. The bilingual pun translates as an English stutter. "The world is no more (no stronger)." Waldrop's version trips over the repeated negation as over the memory of the missing French and German. No… no… No longer… no stronger… Not French… not German. The circuit is broken, but the hiatus is charged with relation. The target language quakes with the transferred load. "The stutter cuts and can reestablish the current," Daive recalls Celan saying. "[It] is in itself an outlet of current, but also a draft of air in our current of life."

* * *

That current: Celan and Daive chuckle, with varying degrees of irony and bemusement during their walking-talking (their acts of regarding, reading, translating), noting that the name for one of those trees whose overhanging leaves "dome" them—paulownia—echoes and is echoed by the names of a cast of characters who star in a partly literal, part-metaphorically-extended family drama contracted to play,

Night and Day, on and around the Contrescarpe. There, beneath those paulownias, we discover at least three Pauls: Celan himself; Daive's mother Paula; and other Paulas further back in Daive's family line, whose literal and metaphorically paved-over histories of violence (the family business was actually the laying of paving stone) underlies one layer of what the 24-year-old Daive, meeting the 45-year-old Celan, has been trying to come to terms with. Daive has been attempting to move from a gnawing past trauma that, he hints, involved the suffering of incestuous abuse, toward something like a whited-out version of it—but with the notion of groping his way toward what can begin to be named, counted, known: toward what may still *look* blank, *blanché*, but might also begin to reveal its score, its number, its decimal place, its value or meaning.

Daive's supercharged receptivity to Celan—to the person, the poet and his poetry, the history the poetry takes in and makes audible, visible, sensed—is clearly, to Celan, exceptional. Elliptically at first, then with a clarity resulting from intensified echoing, *Under the Dome* lets us know that Daive becomes exponentially more aware that his struggle to gain further capacity to see that whited-out decimal place of suffering, is being transferentially inked-in through habitual viewing of what's seemingly ever-present beneath Celan's *fingernails*. For Celan's nails are often—are usually—"black with earth beneath them." Celan "digs" his way across the Contrescarpe and Paris itself; his digging gives us, Daive indicates, not only the poems, but what we'll finally take away as the earth-materials, the matter of time or history: Celan's; Daive's; that of the poems they write and translate, the poetic and sociopolitical histories they share—all of it finally formed into *Under the Dome*.

As he does throughout the book with other recurrent and correlated motifs, Daive is here re-sounding a particular Celan poem, one that, not so coincidentally, concerns poetry's need to risk precisely the danger that conveying brutal subject matter inescapably coagulates with the rush of "getting" what the poem unearths. For the particular poem in question is "There was Earth Inside Them, and/they dug" ("Es war Erde in Ihnen, und/sie gruben"), one of Celan's greatest poems, a kind of sibling of "Death Fugue," whose final stanza—emerging from what's been the maddening-deadly digging of enslaved laborers—risks muting the vast brutality that is the poem's subject matter, simply by seeming to extend through or past that brutality with lines as devastatingly beautiful as any in modern poetry. The poem's final stanza begins with a line whose song sounds out from realms that seem always to have been singing before we ever arrived on the scene, on any scene:

> O one, o none, o no one, o you:
> [O einer, o keiner, o niemand, o du:]
> Where did the way lead when it led nowhere?
> O you dig and I dig, and I dig towards you,
> and on our finger awakes the ring.[11]

What's the price of unearthing truths that emerge only with such digging, and of having made and shared the song, the lyric music that cuts into torture-filled earth to emerge singing?

> I have hidden the blood. What do you think? I have
> paid… I have paid… —I have hidden the madness…
> My poetry masks the madness…

So Daive quotes Celan murmuring, in painful reflection, in a kind of self-torture that makes the word *ambivalent* utterly inadequate. This acknowledgment counts as among *Under the Dome*'s most searing, honest, ambiguous moments. Song of such caliber is what digs up "dust," "sand," what Celan calls "the thorn" that, among other things, is always for him "the camp": always there, with a history at once long, recent, and present (if anyone chooses really to encounter what its presence now is, what it now means). What the poem thus "requires"—to make us need and *want* such subject matter, Celan tells Daive—is nothing less than "an availability that is scorching."[12]

From another vantage point, this partakes of the "doubleness" of poetic speech, which "doubles the world," Celan says. The poem seeks, among other things, to be known as what "denounces" that which has unjustly *been*; equally, it "announces" the *more* that *could* be seen and told: about what *has* existed, and what could be made *to* exist. Daive in the same vein records Celan brooding: "—Passing. Is resemblance the passing of the world, the place, abyss or death of the world?... —Passing: does it mean keeping what is destroyed?" Daive records as well the astounding formulation about Kafka's superposing of form, his tension-filled layering, that Celan ventures elsewhere in *Under the Dome*: Kafka writes the "yes" and the "no" not with two hands, but "with two pencils in one and the same hand." The phrase can't help but make us hear anew the braiding of "yes" and "no" that appears in Celan's early poem "Speak You Also" ("Sprich Auch Du"), an address to the poet, to the reader, of the poem to itself:

> Speak—
> But keep yes and no unsplit.
> And give your say this meaning:
> give it the shade.[13]

Daive—as a poet-translator—doesn't limit himself to the role of witness. He senses that what's involved here is his relation *with* Celan (Celan as person, poet, older friend, mentor; but also the work of translating the poetry together with Celan), as well as Celan becoming taken with Daive's first volume, the book-length poem *Décimale blanche*, seeing in it a profound micro-experience of catastrophe undergone and stammeringly articulated, albeit with gestures toward that world of history more palpably present in Celan's poetry. The status of their relationship changes as Celan decides that he needs to translate *Décimale blanche* into German, even as he makes plans with the poet, translator, and editor André du Bouchet to shepherd the manuscript of *Décimale blanche* into publication.[14]

Under the Dome, written after the passage of time, becomes an understanding reached experientially, in and as—but also as a memoir of—the process of poetic form, a form that includes our reading of it. It recounts Daive's retrospectively deeper understanding of how much was conveyed in Celan's first assessment to him of *Décimale blanche*—and in translating the poem into German as *Weisse Dezimale*—namely, that Celan "loved [the] impalpable concrete-abstract nature" of *Décimale blanche*. "The tale is merciless, familiarly merciless… [with the] density of observation—haunted observation…" *Under the Dome* proves to be an understanding—first Celan's, more slowly, Daive's, then that of the book itself, and then our own—of what *Décimale blanche* was: how its stretching of modern lyric poetry's musical abstraction could yield concrete revelation. This is not a new idea for Celan: it's what real poetry does to make reality, to make history, available to us. But the newness is always in poetry's exploration of the ways to sing the more in reality that has always taken place. To come back full circle to at least one of our circles or domes: it was what justified the "new" that Rothenberg understood—from the poets themselves—necessitated that 1959 title *New Young German Poets*.

The complexity of what Celan hears, sees, in Daive's poetry—an abstract concrete that is not only philosophically but sensorially alive—cannot be "unsplit" from a problem that bedeviled Celan from the start: the charge of making a poetry so difficult that it becomes inaccessible. Celan's stance was that the form's difficulty was not willful, not even willed. Rather, it was exactly as simple—and as complex—as the subject matter, the materials, themselves: any "extra" difficulty would be irrelevant, narcissistic distraction; any less would miss the mark and fail to construct the forms that would be the expression of the historical materials, the experience of them. *Under the Dome* adds something immeasurable in value to the discussion, sheerly through the intensity and depth of Daive's engagement, the profundity of his insight and response to the poetry.[15]

* * *

As Celan had sensed it would, *Décimale blanche* (1967) became a landmark in post-World War II poetry after being initially championed and shepherded into publication by Celan and André du Bouchet. Elliptical yet urgent, searching for aesthetic modalities capable of recovering and giving voice to fragments of unnamed historical traumas both individual and collective, *Décimale blanche* reimagines and extends lyric, surrealist experimental forms, casting them anew together with the poet's own innovations.[16]

Two years after *Décimale blanche* appeared in France, the American expatriate poet, translator, and editor Cid Corman translates *Décimale blanche* and publishes the translation in its entirety under the title *White Decimal*, as issue #13 of his poetry journal *Origin*. Among *Origin*'s readers is the American modernist poet Lorine Niedecker. In the immediately preceding years, Niedecker had felt blocked in her work, in ways that were hardly mysterious to her, for they involved the political strictures against the Left lyric surrealism that had been one of her inspirations and sources early in her career. The difficulty caused for her by those censures were not only their source in the Marxian politics and poetics from which she'd emerged as a poet; they were also supercharged in being propagated by her former lover, fellow poet, and dictatorial pronouncer of truths Louis Zukofsky, who inveighed against the—in his eyes—formally and politically suspect brew of lyricism and surrealism.

Then Niedecker reads Corman's translation of *Décimale blanche* and is knocked out, for in *Décimale blanche* she'd found "the something else I know exists in poetry—that I've been waiting for": "for me this is it," "the height of poetry": "nothing new matters after Daive." Predictably, Zukofsky tells her by letter that Daive's work was sloppy soup that she shouldn't attend to; she struggled with his opinion and then, didn't listen, writing Cid Corman at length about Daive's irresistible "music" that made her know she could really begin to write the poetry she wanted. What might next have happened—for Niedecker, and for American poetry—we can't know, because "then she died."[17]

Made aware, through the years following her 1970 death, of Niedecker's response to the translation of *Décimale blanche*, Daive makes a pilgrimage to Niedecker's Fort Atkinson, Wisconsin home, visits the museum dedicated to her, and then writes—partly as an experiment in what Niedecker might have sounded like had she lived on and, perhaps, been at least a bit French—*Une femme de quelques vies* (2009), which brings Niedecker, and the lyric Surrealist side of American Objectivism, to France in a new way. Keeping the circuit going, Daive then asks Norma Cole to translate the book: it's published as *a woman with several lives* (2012), in a way that lets Niedecker be Niedecker, American, but also, somehow French—so that the translation of Daive has the uncanny effect of sounding like Niedecker's English-language poetry playing with a French it's discovering the possibilities of. It's but a step for Daive to translate Cole's *14000 Facts* and *More Facts* together as *Avis de faits et de méfaits* (2014) and another step to Daive's request that Cole make a new translation of *Décimale blanche*, published as *White Decimal* in 2017.[18]

It's almost a crime—but one that should be committed—to add: Celan's music, of necessity, haunts everywhere throughout this story.

It *needn't* be referentially known, but it happens that Daive's first encounter with one of Niedecker's staunchest advocates, Robert Creeley, occurs soon after Celan's suicide. André du Bouchet tells the devastated Daive that he must work, now more than ever. What should he do, what can he do? Read an American poet named Robert Creeley; the work is very different than Paul's, but there's something in the approach to how poetry both inhabits and departs from the ways language speaks that is not only in Celan. Daive, reluctant at first, follows up on Du Bouchet's suggestion; the result is a decades-long interchange, including Daive's French translations of Creeley. No doubt it can seem—in these interchanges—that "nothing halts": Daive's *Paul Celan: les jours et les nuits* (translated by Cole as *Paul Celan: Days and Nights*) will appear later this year from Duration Press.[19]

Intriguingly, though, the "late 1960s and soon thereafter" period of reception in the U.S. overlaps with Celan's reception elsewhere in the Americas. The reasons are not always, to put it mildly, happy. Only the most obvious is the 1970s–80s era of U.S.-backed military dictatorships of more or less pronounced neo-fascist leanings. Poets and other artists turn often to Celan. They do so not to seek a model, but rather in an interchange of equals, to see what resources in Celan's grappling with what it meant to make poems after the genocide, might aid them.

In Uruguay, in Perú, perhaps especially in Brazil, Argentina, and Chile, and in very distinct ways, Guatemala and México, poets from the late 1970s on, and especially after the increasing dissemination of Celan in Spanish and Portuguese in the 1980s and '90s, notably began working in conversation with Celan. In Chile, for example, poets active in the clandestine-under-Pinochet group CADA (Colectivo Acciones de Arte) made consistent recourse to Celan. Key among them was—and continues to be—Raúl Zurita, whose questions about what in Celan is generative for Latin American experience have proved revelatory. In Argentina, after its mid-'80s restoration of democracy, one of its flagship journals—*Diaro de Poesía*, based in Buenos Aires—was regularly filled with translations of Celan, and with numerous essays on his work and related matrices (not least, what might be gleaned for contemporary Latin America from the "poetry after Auschwitz" debates).[20]

Elsewhere in the Americas, the Martinican poet Monchoachi in his address of acceptance of the Prix Max Jacob, 2003, made explicit what many had seen in his great predecessor Martinican poets Aimé Césaire and Édouard Glissant: a dialogue with Celan that's become a decisive part of the way Celan's various legacies are now articulated:

The "first word" is the word that the poet attempts to restore in a universe deafened by the din of massive destruction, all the languages [*langages*] relentless in their desertifying of the world. The "first word" is quite simply the word. And the poet a warrior, the greatest of warriors, because—to take up the words of Celan, words of a burning timeliness—"exposed in that previously unforeseen sense, and thereby frighteningly in the open [*auf das unheimlichste im Freien*], the poet goes to language with his entire being, sore with reality and seeking reality."[21]

Similarly, in the United States, especially from the 1990s on, the work of poets and artists of color is as integral a part of what Celan means for American poetry and art as any other: often more so. Claudia Rankine's immensely influential volume *Citizen*, for example, very purposefully bears the same subtitle—*An American Lyric*—that her previous book, *Don't Let Me Be Lonely*, had carried, a book whose penultimate movement is indeed an urgent conversation with Celan poems. *Citizen*, for its part, sounds out resonances from across Celan's oeuvre as well, and quite possibly from the ways Rankine's ear has seized on the few recordings made of Celan reading his own work in public.[22]

Finally, among the events that have transformed the landscape of U.S. poetry has been the work of Arab-American poets, such as Palestinian-American Fady Joudah; winner of the Yale Younger Poets Prize, and also translator of the Palestinian poet Mahmoud Darwish, Dr. Joudah also happened to have been Darwish's cardiologist. It was no coincidence that in his invaluable Darwish translation published as *The Butterfly's Burden* (2007), Joudah gave us Darwish's brilliant, understandably charged encounter with Celan, with poems whose subject matter Darwish echoed in the luminous interviews he gave in the years shortly before his death.[23]

* * *

At a moment when exceptionally grave sociopolitical and epidemiological crises haven't so much translated as become one another, it's hard to overstate the importance of Celan, of Daive: of City Lights making them available to us anew. We of course allude to the terrible crises—at once political and health—of COVID-19 and ongoing racist violence consuming much of our world as this new edition of *Under the Dome* goes to press. One turns to poetry and poetics, to Daive and Celan—to Daive's *Under the Dome: Walks with Paul Celan*—neither for a preventative vaccine nor a course-of-treatment cure, and that holds whether the dilemma is medical, political, or both. Yet the human—the sociopolitical, ethical, historical—elements of this crisis are capable of being grasped with deeper understanding, awareness, and sense of critical agency through resources made available in this book: in the work it partakes of, further enables, and offers sustenance to.

1 *The Hudson Review*, Volume 10, no. 4 (Winter 1957–58), pp. 558–574. Rothenberg didn't at the time know that two decades earlier, constructing a sophisticated, elegant version of the German Communist Party's cultural hard line, the leftist critic Walter Benjamin had attacked Kästner's poetry for what the famously melancholic Benjamin had the chutzpah to denounce as "Left-Wing Melancholy." See "Left-Wing Melancholy" (1931) and "The Author as Producer" (1934) in Walter Benjamin, *Selected Writings*, vol. 2 [1927–1934], eds. Michael Jennings, Howard Eiland, and Gary Smith (Cambridge, MA: Harvard University Press, 1999), pp. 423–427, 768–782. For further discussion, see Enzo Traverso's important *Left-Wing Melancholia: Marxism, History, and Memory* (New York: Columbia University Press, 2017), and Peter E. Gordon's astute discussion "Mourning in America," http://bostonreview.net/politics/peter-e-gordon-mourning-america.

Celan and Daive's work helps us see that it wasn't the melancholy so much as a poetics of resigned consolation that Benjamin had attacked in Kästner, a consolatory artistic stance inimical to what in *Under the Dome* Celan will admiringly call "the impalpable concrete-abstract" form, the aesthetic of "haunted observation" that animates Daive's—not to mention, Celan's own—poetry.

2 See *New Young German Poets*, Pocket Poets Series Number 11, ed. and trans. Jerome Rothenberg (San Francisco: City Lights Books, 1959); *The Fifties*, Second Issue (1959), p. 44, and Third Issue (1959), pp. 10–19, 58; Tobias Amslinger, *Verlagsautorschaft: Enzensberger und Suhrkamp* (Göttingen: Wallenstein, 2018), pp. 299–300. See too Rothenberg, "Poetry in the 1950s as a Recollection & Reconstruction," paper delivered at "American Poetry in the 1950s" conference, University of Maine, Orono (June, 1996). And see Philip Gerard, "Pound Notes in German Markets: Paul Celan, Usury, and the Postwar Currency of Ezra Pound," *Modernism/Modernity* 27:1 (2020), pp. 125–145, and *Speaking After: Ezra Pound, Paul Celan, and the Modernist Task of Translation* (forthcoming).

3 "Fugue of Death," Alex Gradussov's translation of Celan's "Todesfuge" in *Savacou: A Journal of the Caribbean Artists Movement*

7/8 (1973), pp. 127–28. Gradussov's rendering of Celan was the only translation that appeared in the issue; the brief note he included—about Celan's Jewishness, and the poem's evocation of the genocide—bore a distinct relationship to reflections elsewhere in the issue about how the new Caribbean writers might think back to the 1930s generation of Antillean anti-fascists who'd preceded them. The issue's inclusion of Gradussov's translation anticipates in significant ways the contemporary Martinican poet Monchoachi's gestures toward Celan's work.

4 "A Song from the Structures of Rime Ringing as the Poet Paul Celan Sings," in Robert Duncan, *Ground Work: Before the War/In the Dark* (1987; New York: New Directions, 2006), p. 12. Michael Palmer— himself becoming known, by the 1980s, as among the U.S. poets in dialogue with Celan's work and, not coincidentally, with the figures in French poetry connected to both Celan and Daive—calls Duncan's poem "one of the finest achievements" of modern American poetry, "a masterpiece of elegy, circularity, and negative lyricism," where "the 'I' singing is at once Duncan/Celan, if not some First Person beyond them both"; see the "Introduction" to *Ground Work*, p. xii. That assessment of Duncan applies equally to one of Palmer's own masterpieces, the 37-page sequence *Baudelaire Series* (from 1988's *Sun*) that re-tells a century's fraught social history, woven together with poetry's own historical situations and acts, while tattooing them—in the form of tombstone-shard—with a broken-name-and-numbers sonnet for Celan, located at these conjoined histories' shared absent center. Republished in Michael Palmer, *Codes Appearing: Poems 1977–1988* (New York: New Directions: 2001), pp. 161–196. Among the most influential French poets linked to Celan, Daive, Duncan, and Palmer have been Emanuel Hocquard, Anne-Marie Albiach, and Claude Royet-Journoud. For further discussion, see Robert Kaufman, "Poetry After 'Poetry After Auschwitz,'" in *Art and Aesthetics after Adorno* [Townsend Papers in the Humanities, No.3], ed. Anthony J. Cascardi (Berkeley: Townsend Humanities Center/University of California Press, 2010) pp. 116–181.

See also Rothenberg's journal *Poems from the Floating World Vol. 1* (1959), pp. 11–12.

5 Rothenberg, "Conclusion" to "Poetry in the 1950s as a Recollection & Reconstruction."

6 Among the first English-language translations of Daive's poetry to appear was expatriate American poet, translator, and editor Cid Corman's translation of the entirety of Daive's book-length poem *Décimale blanche* (Mercure de France, 1967), published in Issue #13 of Corman's journal *Origin* (April 1969), discussed below. Translations of a selection of Daive's poems appeared in Paul Auster, ed., *The Random House Handbook of Twentieth-Century French Poetry* (New York: Random House, 1982); see also Daive's *A Lesson in Music*, trans. Julie Kalendek (Providence, R.I.: Burning Deck, 1992). For later English translations of Daive's work, and his and Norma Cole's translations of one another, see n. 18 below.

7 Mary Ann Caws' words appear on the back cover of Paul Celan, *Breathturn into Timestead: The Collected Later Poetry—A Bilingual Edition*, translated and with commentary by Pierre Joris (New York: Farrar, Straus, and Giroux, 2014). In Fall 2020, FSG will also publish Joris' translation (again with Joris' commentary) of Celan, *Memory Rose into Threshold Speech: The Collected Earlier Poetry—A Bilingual Edition*.

In addition to Joris' work, the English-language scene has been fortunate to have had, in the decades following Rothenberg's inaugural efforts, invaluable translations of Celan's *Collected Prose* by Rosmarie Waldrop (1986; Carcanet, UK; Routledge, 2003) and translations of the poetry by Joachim Neugroschel, Michael Hamburger, John Felstiner, Nikolai Popov and Heather McHugh, and Susan H. Gillespie, among others—as well as the tireless championing not only of the aesthetic but also political importance of Celan-translations by poetry-world artists, editors, and activists such as the late Benjamin Hollander, who quickened interest in Celan at an important moment with his editing of "Translating Tradition: Paul Celan in France," *Acts 8/9* (1988). J.M. Coetzee thoughtfully discusses and gives full citations to the work of most of the English translators mentioned above; see "Paul Celan and his translators" in Coetzee, *Inner Workings: Literary Essays 2000–2005* (London: Penguin, 2007), pp. 114–131; the exceptions are Neugroschel's translation of Celan, *Speech-Grille and Selected Poems* (New York: E.P. Dutton, 1971) and Gillespie's translation and commentary *Corona: Selected Poems of Paul Celan* (Barrytown, NY: Station Hill, 2013).

8 Celan, *The Meridian*, eds. Bernard Böchenstein and Heino Schmull, with assistance from Michael Schwartzkopf and Christiane Wittkop, trans. and with a Preface by Pierre Joris (Stanford: Stanford University Press, 2011), p. 73.

9 Quoted from Pierre Joris, introductory essay to the *Poets of the Millennium* series: Paul Celan, *Selections*, ed. and intro by Pierre Joris (Berkeley: University of California Press, 2005), p. 26.

10 Henri Meschonnic, "On appelle cela traduire Celan," *Les Cahiers du chemin no. 14*, January 1972, pp. 148–149.

11 *Poems of Paul Celan, Revised and Expanded,* trans., with an Introduction and Postscript, by Michael Hamburger (New York: Persea, 2002), pp. 130–131. In the German original: "O einer, o keiner, o niemand, o du:/ Wohin gings, da's nirgendhin ging?/O du gräbst und ich grab, und ich grab mich dir zu,/und am Finger erwacht uns der Ring."

12 To follow the idea a few steps further: Refusing consolation, Celan's poetry had aimed not to pretend to redeem or return to life the millions murdered, but rather to bring to our engagement with the poetry the particularities of loss that those irrevocable mass murders entail. Yet in its lightning-like power to galvanize our experiential awareness *of* all this, the poetry paradoxically also threatens—against its own intentions—to mask history's madness when we may somehow come to feel that what the poem evokes is even faintly akin to having brought the dead *back to life* (a redemptive delusion that would deny rather than make available what Celan had designated as "that which happened" [*dass, was geschah*]).

13 *Poems of Paul Celan*, trans. Hamburger, "Speak You Also," pp. 68–69. In the original German: "Sprich—/Doch scheide das Nein nicht vom Ja./Gib deinem Spruch auch den Sinn:/gib ihm den Schatten."

14 As a result of Du Bouchet's and Celan's active involvement, excerpts from *Décimale blanche* were published in the influential literary journal *L'Éphémère* (co-edited by Du Bouchet, Celan, Yves Bonnefoy, and others). Du Bouchet then saw *Décimale blanche* through to book-publication with the eminent press Mercure de France in 1967.

15 One crucial instance: Daive retells Celan's reading him the recently composed (1967) "You lie in the great listening" ("Du liegst im großen Gelausche"), *Breathturn into Timestead,* pp. 322–323 (final word in the poem's translation emended, at the end of this note 15, from "stalls" to "halts"). The poem quickly became a *locus classicus* of Celan's purported obscurity. Its imaged allusions to the 1919 murders of German revolutionaries Rosa Luxemburg and Karl Liebknecht—by the proto-Nazi *Freikorps* irregulars who'd soon contribute toward formation of the *Sturmabteilung* (the SA, Nazi Stormtroopers), and who threw the assassinated communist leaders into the waters of Berlin's Spree and Havel rivers and the parallel Landwehr canal—cross with symbols taken from the 1944 executions of the German army conspirators who failed in their attempt to assassinate Hitler; all are folded into the poem's venturing of a listened-for solidarity that reads as partial death wish. Daive's account cuts through decades of polemics about whether the images and allusions are comprehensible—thus, whether or not the poem is available—to anyone not knowing its historical referents: "'—And I have written this poem... right?' He speaks to me at length about the murders of Rosa Luxemburg and Karl Liebknecht with the same intensity as when he speaks of his parents shot in the concentration camp."

That *intensity* Daive identifies reappears as the force field that the poem formally constellates around the *loss* of the historical agents it elliptically references. "Du liegst" ("You lie") generates a semblance experience in which loss and historical knowledge coincide. The charged co-inciding is the intensity carried over to readers who may not know the "facts" but sense—from the formal working up of particularized emotions and experiences of loss—precisely what lies murkily in the poem's "great listening" to what's *lost* in history. It's not that Daive's account is to be externally imposed onto the poem, or offered as evidence of how it "should" be read. Rather, Daive suggests that what the poem's form is charged with passes to readers who, perhaps lacking the historical specifics, nonetheless experience the poem as eliciting in them the sense that the missing referents stand precisely for what's been lost through violent erasure. "Nothing/halts," this river poem ends, its last line-break halting at, yet continuing with—even while surging past—the specificity of the sedimented, superposed histories that move in time's current towards us.

16 The abstraction and concretion—separate, moving towards one another—inaugurate the poem with familiar yet new experiments in what Mallarméan blank space had permitted, from the poem's first line, "white decimal," separated by most of a blank page from the second line, "at the edge of space," until, by the final two pages, the need to find precision and palpability in what had seemed faint if even present becomes the sensing of a history all too filled with heretofore unknown suffering that one might—understandably, mistakenly—blame on the act of formal aesthetic reflection that's made it visible: "she says/absent/she was one of the three glimmers/resting in spite of the cold/far from the window and the lamp//she says/she haunted what absence no longer holds/the glimmer/that held it before her/she felt from it a moment of unknown pain/at absolving the lamp and the window[.]"

Jean Daive, *White Decimal*, trans. Norma Cole (Oakland: Omnidawn, 2017), pp. 11, 70–71; 77, 136–137; original French text published as *Décimale blanche* (Paris: Mercure de France, 1967).

17 Grace Paley, "Mother," in *The Collected Short Stories* (New York: Farrar, Straus, and Giroux, 2007). For extended treatment of Niedecker's later career, her discovery of Daive's work, and the aftermaths for American and French poetry, see Kaufman, "Lorine Niedecker's French Revolution" (forthcoming).

18 Jean Daive, *Une femme de quelques vies* (Paris: Flamarion, 2009); *a woman with several lives* (Iowa City and Paris: La Presse, 2012); Norma Cole, *14000 Facts* (Davis, CA: a+bend press, 2009) and *More Facts* (Montréal: Tente, 2009), both translated by Jean Daive as *Avis de faits et de méfaits* (Paris: Éditions Corti, 2014).

19 See citations to and discussion of "You lie in the great listening" ["Du liegst im großen Gelausche"] in n.15 above. And see Daive, *Paul Celan: les jours et les nuits*, Afterword by Werner Hamacher (Paris: Nous, 2016); trans. Norma Cole as *Paul Celan: Days and Nights* (Duration Press, forthcoming 2020).

20 Visiting City Lights' offices after Bay Area readings in April 2016—in which those connections had been central—Zurita referred to *New Young German Poets* having been produced there, in the building; at a

get-together afterwards he thanked the press's staff for the legacy, and said, of the office, "Sentí que aquella poesía estara en el cuarto" ("I felt that that poetry was in the room"). For further discussion see Kaufman, "Il faut continuer... d'être absolument moderne: Adorno's Modernism Now, Zurita's Lyric After," *Constelaciones: Revista de Teoría Crítica* 11 (2020).

It's important here to also mention the work of the world-renowned Afro-Colombian sculptor and installation artist Doris Salcedo. For Salcedo's work, the Celan connection has been crucial, moving with her into the making of concrete-poem sculptures, and in related works she's described as meditations on histories of systemic violence and racism. Many of Salcedo's works have taken their titles from Celan poems. See *Doris Salcedo*, eds. Julio Rodrigues Widholm and Madeleine Grynstejn (Chicago: University of Chicago Press, 2015).

21 Monchoachi, "Speech on the Acceptance of the Prix Max Jacob" (2003); we are indebted to Brent Hayes Edwards' essay—and the generous handing over of its final movement to his translation of Monchoachi—"The Specter of Interdisciplinarity," *PMLA* 123:1 (January, 2008), pp. 188–194.

22 Claudia Rankine, *Don't Let Me Be Lonely: An American Lyric* (St. Paul, MN: Graywolf, 2004), pp. 61, 97, 130–131, 143, 149, 154. Rankine, *Citizen: An American Lyric* (St. Paul, MN: Graywolf, 2014).

23 See Mahmoud Darwish, *The Butterfly's Burden*, trans. Fady Joudah (Port Townsend, WA: Copper Canyon, 2007); "Interview with Mahmoud Darwish: On the Possibility of Poetry in a Time of Siege" in *Mahmoud Darwish, Exile's Poet: Critical Essays*, ed. Hala Khamis Nassar and Najat Rahman (Northampton, MA: Olive Branch Press, 2008), pp. 319–326; Fady Joudah, *Footnotes in the Order of Disappearance: Poems* (Minneapolis, MN: Milkweed Editions, 2018).

Under the Dome

No matter whom, no matter what, Paul Celan reads no matter where because the word drives him to memory and is the imaginary space where the legibility of the world is acted out.

At the end of his life he finds in the North German vocabulary a more faithful mirror of his memory where a—wild—etymology forms with utmost acuity and violence.

A recollection: near Avenue Emile-Zola, Paul Celan looks for a grocery store. He buys a lightbulb that he puts in a huge netbag. Carrying the netted lightbulb he moves on in a lordly way. And the net hangs heavy.

The world is illegible and the matter of words engenders a structure: the poem. Vibration of sense used as energy.

Often a word is the starting point. As if a man come from the East could read the illegible world with a vocabulary most radically alien to him.

A great listener, with close attention. But Paul Celan does not exclude floating language. What he sets afloat within language?

He reads the newspapers, all of them, technical and scientific works, posters, catalogues, dictionaries and philosophy.

A recollection: Lesieur Oil.

He reads Rilke, Trakl, Kafka, Heidegger. Listens to conversations, notes a word heard in a store, in the street. He reads Meister Eckhart.

He reads no matter where (posters, the placard for Lesieur Oil mounted on a van driving by). He focuses his mirror on difference, opposition. The word, for a moment, focuses memory.

"A poet is a pirate," he says often.

He reads Margarete Susmann, her book on Kafka. He reads Martin Buber. Manuals on driving trucks, cars. Traffic rules.

The matter of words. Words as matter. Distance within logic.

Coming back from London, Paul Celan tells me that he has seen God under the door: "A ray of light in my hotel room."

I repeat to myself:

tagnächtlich
die Bärenpolka:[1]

forever,
the bear polka:
all life long,
the bear polka:

till the end of time,
the bear polka:

Walking in Rue d'Ulm (in May 68) Paul Celan says to me: "Last night I heard something like distant cannons."

Reading the posters around the square of the Luxembourg: "Only the One exists," "We are all German Jews," "It is forbidden to forbid." Paul Celan has a mocking smile...

"The world is uninhabited," he says on the terrace of the Panthéon, "the moon already is."

Avenue Emile-Zola: the empty apartment he has occupied for a week now. In the bathroom he bends over the tub, dips his left hand in the water: underwear floats up. Laundry. "You'll excuse my finishing the laundry?" With his smile.

In a gray coat he crosses the Place du Palais-Royal. He suddenly stops under the thick snow. He seems unsure which way to go. He turns his head and walks on. He is going to cross the Seine.

I am watching him. He does not see me.

Rue de Richelieu: "Friends are the first to turn on you, don't forget that," he tells me.

As for God, quoting Kafka:
"Sometimes yes, sometimes no."

Psychiatric Hospital. The long tables in the refectory of Sainte-Geneviève-des-Bois.

Games of approach between Paul Celan, Joerg Ortner, and me. Which?

"I gave your book to Joerg Ortner to read, an Austrian painter," he says one evening. Later he tells me: "The Austrian painter I mentioned, whom I gave your book, very much liked *Décimale blanche*... right..."[2]

Joerg Ortner's black hat. At the cemetery of Thiais. The day of Paul Celan's funeral.

Chapter of translations.
Apropos *Windgalle* and *Treckschutenzeit*.[3]
  Wind gall   Bargetrekking time

All the words are composites. The second term always the most important. The verb is tied to the second term. There is a vertical sense.

Paul Celan chews a word like a stone. All day long. It produces word-energy. It all goes into the energy of his composite words. Here we have his biography.

Paul Celan invites the reader to travel inside the word (voyage, labyrinth).

On the one hand, the composite noun—on the other, no verb is given. Paul Celan does not give the verb.

Morphology.

Paul Celan's joy on discovering a word—*Windgalle*. He burrows into words.

Is there somebody in the word?

The word is no more,
The world is no more (no stronger).

I have to carry you.

Absence of the verb: the verb is absorbed into the energy of the composite noun.

Morphology.

Paul Celan walks looking at the ground. Lifts his head to note certain places. Lifts his head for example on the Place des Patriarches and looks toward the Public Baths, the *Bains-Douches.*

Recollection: Paul coming back from London. "I have seen God, I have heard God: a ray of light under the door of my hotel room." And later Paul recalls Kafka's formulation, "Sometimes God, sometimes nothing."

Eternity present in Rue d'Ulm. In his office. In the garden. Near the pool.

Eternity is gray (Paul Celan).

Eternity is useless. It is called way stations of the century.

Paul walks with his hands crossed in back.

To recollect a Sunday we spent together. Took the bus as far as the Opéra. The Saint-Lazare area. The theater. Then went into a café where Paul notices a woman sitting among the crowd. Her face drawn. Pale. He falls back, as if frightened. Pushes me. We rush out. In the street he tells me. "Her face reminded me of a friend who died."

High alert during all our encounters.

Paul staring at my tie.

The gray coat. The gray coat's presence. Ample. The London type.

High forehead and gray coat.

His watch. The importance of the watch.

I should talk of what was no longer Paul. Seeing him in the hospital. The long table of the refectory. Gisèle and me and a voluble Paul.

Paul's wife, Gisèle. And the twin rings on their fingers.

The psychiatric hospital of Sainte-Geneviève-des-Bois.

The refectory, the dormitory. Paul's.

The refectory, the halls, the white metal gurneys on wheels.

The wind, the wind, the kite.

The venison stew Paul treated me to after my poems were published in German in the Zürich newspaper.

La Chope. Name pronounced with thirst and appetite. "Let's eat at La Chope," he'd say.

Basically no eyes for things. In the street, no eyes.

"Jean Daive, what is your task?" He asks me this question in Rue Gay-Lussac, near the Geographic Institute. Silence. Long silence. We cross the street. We're on the other sidewalk. He puts his hands in his pockets. It is mild. Autumn. Yes. Autumn. "Your task, Jean Daive!"

I look at myself and within myself I look at Gisèle. I write this today. Gisèle.

There is no reply possible. To look at him, a matter of great sweetness, great attention.

Rue d'Ulm as lair and landmark.

Side by side, translating "Engführung," "Stretto," at the Royal Panthéon. On his right.

At Paul's burial, in the car. Gisèle's hand. Her wedding ring.

Her wet eyes. Her lips. And in the crowd, tall, the man with the black hat: Joerg Ortner.

The laurel wreath. The funeral wreath, severe and perfect, brought from Vienna to Paris by Klaus Demus[4] (on his lap).

The brutal shock of his disappearance. I "see" the jump into the Seine. I can see it. And I see again his laundry soaking in the tub Avenue Emile-Zola, his hands stirring the soapy water. With elegance and determination.

Empty space of the apartment. Empty place. Big bookcase. Empty.

A word while walking. At the crossing of Boulevard Saint-Germain and Boulevard Saint-Michel, going North. The crowd of May 68. Paul looks at faces he's never seen before. As if—this is implied—the crowd should be familiar, always the same.

—The've come out of their holes and don't know they can never go back.

—After the events?

—Yes, after.

What is this sudden remembrance of Paul, so intense that I dream, this Saturday, March 25, 1989, of Gisèle. In front of this store. In the street. I look at her and she knows I'm going to ask her to tell me everything. (Which she has done already.)

Paul Celan—his failed suicide in the small room of Rue de Longchamp. The blood. Gisèle's composure. Paul's happiness Rue de Longchamp. Paul's frozen happiness there. The daily newspapers, the daily mail, the daily misery, of Germany, of him, of Germany. Germany and German.

The German language lived in Paris. On an island basically and perhaps to be carried, open, in a Great Book with Gisèle, and then without her.

Without ring.

The poem he writes in the street and then telephones to her from a public phonebooth.

I imagine the poems of *Sprachgitter, Speech Grid,* telephoned this way and written along the Seine.

Being incapable of speaking had long made my life impossible when I met Paul Celan, who had written *Sprachgitter* (1959): a grid, language. Not of words or images, but gathering the world into a grid to elucidate it.

Two women (Greta and Olga) preceded and led me to his universe: one of difficult beauty, the other beautiful without strangeness. A third would come.

The game of translation makes a grid appear before my eyes. The way an innermost secret slowly becomes clear, can become clear to us.

How could a grid contain madness?

Being incapable of articulating an absence behind absence plunges me into a life—a non-life. Everything implies deduction, and the grid authoritatively puts it in place.

Language has begun to dim like a lamp, and I am walking in the snow one January morning when I meet two women.

The grid holds suffering that will writhe in a convulsive drama.

How could a grid worry about the locus of a language it steeps in a final emulsion?

Syntax torments the narrative that words cannot untangle.

There is always a story or an idea to tell. A story means progression, means torment.

A word turns like a sun. Mirrored fullness that blinds words.

On Paul's right, at a table in the Royal Panthéon. Silence. He looks at me, smiling:
—Would you translate me?

—You know that is difficult!
—I know it is difficult, but I will help you.
—Alright.

A little later, on Paul Celan's right, at a table in the Royal Panthéon—the same one—we start to work on translating "Engführung."
—A word is a word and translating me means finding always the right word (apropos the series of botanical terms: granulous, fibrous, stemmed, compact, racemose and radial, reniform, lamellate and palmate, porous, runcinate). Sometimes you have to let the sense drift. And then you must immediately go back to the beginning, to the literal meaning: it is the right one.

At the crossing of Rue des Écoles and Boulevard Saint-Michel, Paul Celan asks me:
—Have you thought of writing in another language?
—No. Have you?
—Yes, sometimes, in French... But it's not possible.
—Why?
He smiles.

Apropos the first two lines of "Engführung," *Verbracht ins / Gelände:* what he authorizes with a violent stroke across the paper becomes:
Dé–porté dans l'étendue.

—You sometimes have to shift the meaning of a stanza, but find its balance, he says.

A poetry born of illness.

Subjects and conversations: the scandal ("Todesfuge," "Death Fugue": I immediately became the target of the antisemites... no... I became the target of all of Germany")—nazism—deportation—the scandal: the plagiarism affair, how it wounded him:[5] "It's a conspiracy"—the carpenter Zimmer—Hölderlin's tower—intransigence—guilt—friendship betrayed—Antschel, Ancel, Celan—the Neckar—work camps—the Bukovina—the plagiarism affair: "An outrage"—Auschwitz and poetry: "Man will continue to talk, man will continue to bear witness with or without Adorno"—the camp (two lines, the one on the left, the one on the right, and changing lines)—public readings— Gisèle—Nicolas de Staël—Giacometti ("Sometimes one has to be worldly like Giacometti")—*The Ephémère*[6]—André du Bouchet—Ezra Pound—the Kabbala—Meister Eckhart— Rosa Luxemburg—Paris—the Seine—the Contrescarpe— Walking in the Luxembourg Gardens—Rue du Pot-de-Fer— Rue Tournefort (on the threshold his ritual formula: "I won't ask you in because my cleaning woman didn't come today")—"I want to translate you: I want to translate *Décimale blanche*... right"—Heidegger—Visiting me in Rue Coquillière: "This is a real poet's place"—Rue de Longchamp—Berlin—Avenue Emile-Zola—the Russian Revolution—Mandelstam—Peter Handke—Prague—Hölderlin—Klaus Demus—Vienna—Tristan Tzara—May 68—We are all German Jews—Nelly Sachs— Daniel Cohn-Bendit.[7]

How do I remember Paul today, twenty years later?

And how did this immediate triangulation happen so naturally? Paul—Gisèle—me.

There is much silence in this, so much that remains unsaid. I'm still dumbfounded, even today.

Nevertheless many trips: London, Venice, Jerusalem, Amsterdam, Antibes.

His meeting Martin Flinker on the Pont-Neuf. Paul become a different man. Knowing everything about Germany and knowing everybody. Every writer and every publisher.

At a table in the back of the Greek restaurant in Rue de l'École-de-Médecine, Paul is writing in his notebook. A plate of tarama, paper, and a fork. Writing, on a corner of the table. Cold and self-contained. He does not see me. Does not feel my presence. I leave.

The chestnut trees. Chestnuts. Light rain falling between us, between the leaves. He tells me he expects a telegram from Germany. Sadly, tiredly.

All the things he does not tell me and all the things I know from Gisèle. All the secret whispers of a man and a woman, transmitted secretly.

To describe his face: contorted—smiling—hurt—judgmen-tal—lordly—generous—nostalgic—imperious—contorted—luminous—childlike—severe.

Paul calls me. He has finished his translation of *Décimale blanche*. He worked during Christmas vacation. He wants me to clarify the meaning of certain words. He asks me to explain "*voix pivotale*," and finally "*énoncé*": "What does *énoncé* mean?"[8] The word will remain untranslated.

It is over this untranslated word that I meet Joerg Ortner, who asks:

—What does *énoncé* mean?[8]

We are meeting in the Place des Vosges. Paul Celan is dead.

We are working at his big table in Avenue Emile-Zola. He is very concentrated, very precise. He loves words. He erases them as if they should bleed.

The last phone call: his voice somber, tormented, hollow. It actually trembles, and I am filled with terror.
—Jean Daive, I don't see you any more. Why? Almost sobbing. We talk. We must see each other. We make an appointment for Avenue Emile-Zola. Two days later, nothing. Nobody. Paul Celan has disappeared.

On Monday morning of April 20, 1970, Gisèle on the phone:
—Jean, did you see Paul on Sunday? No? I'm worried. I'm without news. Paul has disappeared.

My distress afterwards. Lasts and lasts. A month of emptiness, of anguish. Of no solid ground. Days absolutely empty. I feel his death in me as a break with the human world. With language.

I can imagine the night, the Seine, the Pont Mirabeau perhaps, no doubt (the bridge already named in his poems). A Sunday.

And Gisèle. Day after day during the wait, the disappearance, the flight, the going away, the lack of signs.

Day after day. In tears, on my birthday. At the Vagenende There and elsewhere. Lost in Paul's death.

One evening, Gisèle:

—I am going to the morgue to identify Paul.

The evening after:

—He was unrecognizable. The face puffed up and black.

And a little earlier:

—Jean, Paul's body has been fished out of the Seine. At the last sluice-gate.

While Paul is missing Gisèle says to me:

—Paul left his watch on his night table. So Paul is dead.

—Ah? Why?

—Paul always kept his watch on his wrist. He told me: the day I take off my watch I'll have decided to die.

So Gisèle knew.

The Aegean Sea is in front of me. Against my table and beyond my book, pines, waves breaking on the sand. The Aegean is a wound. I never talk of it. It is blue, transparent, I see it. I don't see the wound.

A man digs in front of a stone wall white as a sepulchre: it's a low house set deep in the ground, without window or door, and I can't help thinking of my father's vanishing into thin air.

I no longer know or simply don't know what vanished with him. But he left an infinity of presumptions and my mother's vengeance.

The island is still calm on this late afternoon. I watch a donkey immobile enough to disenchant the stony landscape.

Why bring the donkey into the wound? The island is calm and flat and silent and yet all I look at is convex. The donkey, the spade, the wave, the sepulchre, all these moments lived in and held against the sky come back to me whereas they should dig down into another vanishing.

I think of Paul Celan. I am in a beautiful house overlooking the blue sea. Edith listens as I tell her for the first time of my father. I think of Paul Celan. I am in a beautiful white house. I think of the books he gave me and the moments surrounding them, always highly charged. One of them comes back to me:

A golden light fills his office in Rue d'Ulm. We have just had lunch. We are in a good mood.

—I am going to give you, he says, the *Sonnets* of Shakespeare that I have translated. I just received copies. They are love poems addressed probably—according to the specialists—to a young man he had loved.... Read sonnet LVII.

He is sitting at the table. He looks at me gravely. Inscribes the book.

[...]

March 1968. I remember. I was going to do some shopping with my netbag and cry under the paulownias. Impossible to be. Impossible to write. I was a brain-cry[9] that could not be expressed. Some fragments came about that I showed to Paul at his request ("You write, Jean Daive?—Yes—Show me!"), Paul's tone authoritative, even imperious. I showed him. "I like very much how you write, Jean Daive. I would like to translate you some day and I'd like to translate these poems for a Swiss journal." Which he did.

But I want to remember more precisely, juxtapose these two moments. March 1968. My absolute solitude and anxiety under the paulownias, the shopping bag, and one of our last walks, that is to say, an errand we did together Avenue Emile Zola. Paul very alone, bitter, I should think (a sulfurous solitude), holding a large netbag into which he slips a lightbulb he has just bought.

[…]

A recollection of Gisèle's.
"One whole summer long I repainted the apartment in Rue de Longchamp… (she had chased Paul from this apartment in the 16th arrondissement and above all away from herself) and spending hours on the ladder, I wanted, really wanted to die."

Gisèle is a good storyteller. She has this in common with my mother as well as the same face. Bony, touching, tender, angular, skinny. Gisèle tells me of Paul's failed suicide, the maid's room where she discovered him.

The chestnut tree and the garden of my childhood. Then the chestnuts of the avenues. The leaves, the luminous green, the chestnuts in autumn. A green light above us, domed. Conversation and footsteps. Paul on my left.
—I'm expecting a telegram from Germany.
—Ah.
—I would like to refuse going there.
—Ah.
—I would like to refuse going there.
—Ah.

[…]

Basically Paul's presence takes place for me under the sign of three women: Greta, Olga who make me discover his work, and Gisèle who explains the man to me. An identical cluster groups Greta, Gisèle, Paula. Olga is something else. She is a wife.

Greta in my arms in Vienna and in Paris. I think I am dreaming. A strange and seemingly paradoxical summer in my arms. She reads in the Bibliothèque Sainte-Geneviève. I read in the Bibliothèque nationale. I pick her up every day in the late afternoon. And repeatedly, four times especially, our exchanges upset me. Greta asks:

—What are you reading these days?

—Proust.

A smile. The amused smile of a woman in the know. In the know for two. The first time I did not really understand. Even though I felt ill at ease.

—How strange... because we too have *our* Proust.

—Ah.

—Yes... Robert Musil. (This is in 1958.)

Time passes.

A little later. Same situation: Bibliothèque Sainte-Geneviève. Same walk. Same café or even room.

—What are you reading these days?

—Georges Bataille.

—Who is that?

—A great contemporary philosopher.

A smile. I wait. And sure enough:

—How strange... we too have a great contemporary philosopher.

—Ah.

—Yes... Ludwig Wittgenstein.

Time passes. Same scene.
—What are you reading these days?
—Rimbaud.
—...We too have our Rimbaud.
—Mmmm...
—Yes... Georg Trakl.

Time passes and the scene is not altogether the same. Greta knows I am disturbed and enthusiastic about Ponge. I am looking for first editions of Francis Ponge.
—So you are reading Ponge? (Amused smile.)
—Yes, I'm reading Ponge. He's cleansing.
—Cleansing?
—Yes, he cleanses the language, the words of the language. And the dirty water is not without wit.
—Ah. (Greta says Ah!)
A pause. Then:
—How strange... because we too have a poet who cleanses and scrubs spiritually.
—Ah.
—Paul Celan.

This is the first time I hear the name. From lips I have been kissing.

In Paul Celan, spirituality is made of densities (structures of densities). The densities are superposed. Their meanings are superposed. In Ponge, there is cleansing. And the cumulative cleansings let a spirituality appear "in the negative."

The reader is free to reply: I understand what I am to understand.

Arcades of green light we walk under, often along the greenish surface of the Seine. Static glass and dynamic ribbon. Paul Celan:
—You are going to Prague?
—Yes!
—I'll give you a letter to take to a friend, Franz Wurm.

I am really going to Vienna to meet Greta, then to Prague with her.

Gisèle suspecting something and already expecting the worst. Afterwards she tells me: I walked through Paris for hours calling out: Jean Daive.
Rue de Longchamp: a bourgeois interior. Paul's large bookcase left behind. In the other room that I don't see, a large round table a meter from the double bed. The apartment has seen all of Germany in procession.

In Rue Cujas (we like this street and its corner bookstore), Greta says to me:
—But in Trakl (compared to Paul Celan) there is in addition the dimension of incest, which you should understand perfectly.

Basically, she knows nothing about me (1958).

Monologue. Selfportrait:
—I love four-fruit jam. Ah, yes... Cherries, strawberries, raspberries, currants... Robert Musil—Ludwig Wittgenstein—Georg Trakl—Paul Celan.

Rue d'Ulm. Place de la Contrescarpe. Rue du Pot-de-Fer. Rue Tournefort. I accompany him to where some years later Edith is supposed to move "us." The same courtyard. The same (infernal) echo. Amplifying the world. A cave. Here Paul went out of his mind. Then the police take him to Sainte-Geneviève-des-Bois. A horror. A world out of the Middle Ages.

—Jean Daive, do you know what the nurse says when he comes into the dormitory in the morning:
Debout, les morts! "Up, you corpses!"

Somewhat later in our long conversation orchestrated masterfully by Paul, the virtuoso of composition, of memory (Tzara), of reading (Rilke, Trakl), of daily life (budding friendship among patients), he gives me a plaintive (seductive) look which is not really a reproach (forestalls it in fact):
—Last time you gave me a book: *Testament* by Roger Gilbert-Lecomte.
—Yes.
—I read it carefully.
—Yes.
—My doctor found me reading this book.
—Ah.
—It was a difficult moment for him and me. You are reading a book? he asks. Yes. He picks it up, closes it and reads the title. What? You read a book called *Testament!* How did this get in here? A present from a friend. The doctor leaves, after asking me to stop reading it.

I look at his mocking eyes, his smile. He is delighted to see me dismayed.

When I leave Sainte-Geneviève-des-Bois that I too experience as a prison house, a feeling of freedom washes over me. Between the road and the hospital, a peaceful space, a meadow slopes toward an absence of walls. When I point this out to him:

—No more need for walls, no more need for barbed wire as in the concentration camps. The incarceration is chemical. The prisoner is chemical: he cannot take two steps on his own. But he can look at the outside. He can talk, right...

There is no color in Paul's books (he also never wears colors). But there are all the nuances of white, black, gray.
—Pigeon gray—Paris gray, he says.

Walking on Rue d'Ulm, by the Cinémathèque, he seems to be fighting with himself, hands thrust forward, menacing, convulsive, fingers snapping in the air. Fingers with black nails. Earth underneath.

I often remember his nails with earth under them, as if he were burying, unburying, digging. Struggling with the real? Struggling with the dream of language?

The Place de la Contrescarpe with its paulownias resembles a small village, and he likes the sense of protection this hill gives him.

I see myself again at Sainte-Geneviève-des-Bois. As I enter the space splits in two. On my left a blinding lamp, on the right a butcher's cart piled with saws. At the same time I enter a familiar space from childhood. Stone steps plunge toward the cellar: on the left coal, on the right potatoes. In the middle, in my father's arms, me with bleeding ear and gums. Paul Celan is waiting for me in front of a refectory table.

It is autumn.

Against the wooden stairs, against judgment, Paul braces himself, opens his eyes: sometimes his glance seems to listen.

Sometimes moving forward in the air, searching for air, I find an autumn, golden, impenetrable, what no word can unveil.

I understand: painted angels no longer guard the black holes.

The Contrescarpe as a choked garden. Behind a fence, clochards are tossing empty bottles about that burst in the grass.

We watch.

Gisèle Celan has just told me that Paul has disappeared. Her voice anguished, utterly. She wants to see me, talk to me, tell me, explain.

"Narration torments the syntax." Alain Veinstein comes to see me on Place Saint-Sulpice where I reread the articles of the *Dictionary of Contemporary Works*. He comes to pick up his manuscript "Giornata," which is under consideration at Mercure de France. He notices my anxiety:
—What's wrong?
—Paul Celan has disappeared.
Silence.
—Is there something I can do?

It is autumn. The voices in the street sound golden, float on the air. We walk. An autumn at the end of a chestnut-lined avenue. We cross the Place des Patriarches. He looks toward the Public Baths, the *Bains-Douches*.

He looks at me, smiles. We both smile.
—What's today's laundry, Jean Daive?
—Is there anything left to launder?

We go back up Rue Mouffetard to 45 Rue d'Ulm. His office. He opens the dark blue folder with poems by Klaus Demus.

We work all Sunday.

Around us buzzing, sounds blending into the space. His steps enter it like a legend, lithe.

I may know that our travels on earth are a dream. They must be. Interrupted by the flash of an encounter.

We walk by the chestnut trees. A bleached-out space. Rotten pavement. He walks. I walk. Late afternoon. He is trembling or, more exactly, brooding in strange, stubborn silence. He wants to talk, his lips are trembling, as are his hands. He looks at me. Opens his mouth. Nothing. We walk on. Rue Gay-Lussac. A bus stop. He holds out his hand, pained.

—Pardon me, Jean Daive. I'll take the bus.

There is a transition from the chestnut trees of the child counting leaves to the chestnut trees of the walker counting chestnuts.

Water, the carafe of water, because he is thirsty.

The impenetrable—inhuman—distance between him and the Other. A distance where the remains of the world may accumulate: and I mean the remains.

On his finger, his ring.

Bizarre references in conversation:

—Nowadays, Jean Daive, it takes 1500 francs to buy a pair of shoes (1969).
—Ah.

Truth does not like powder, does not try to reduce to powder. Yet that day snow is falling on us. Enormous flakes thicken the space. The world become opaque turns hard, impossible to interpret.
—Can you see in this, can you, he asks, the ground is dangerously slippery.

I briskly take his arm. He is slipping. He prepares to slip and in falling reads the advertisement on a passing van:
—Lesieur Oil. Ha! Ha! That's too funny!
I hold him firmly by the arm.

The man: seductive and impersonal—the charm of his distance.

Walking can make the change of place euphoric. A step. A step and another step. A step. I walk. I go on. I can plunge my steps into gloom: but the steps break the anxiety, overheat the distance within.

Cosmic dust covers us. The wind lifts the air.
—I'm writing like never before, he says.

Astonished to be writing. Most often astonished not to be writing.
Each day its astonishment.

Autumn made of cranes and cables: geometric tunes around the sky, and us there, askew, explosives double-charged with pallor and stubborn silence, we move on, but—how to put it?—without dodging (I insist), without fail (I insist). So all must be said and all will be. Without sham (I insist).

[…]

Basically, I have a question. When I told him that I wanted to start a magazine, why did he say: I'll give you something. And why—this is the real question—did he give me these two poems: "Ungewaschen," which became "Les Bains-Douches," and "Gold," "L'Or"? (The word *Bains-Douches* supposedly "implicit"—always his distance.)

And why did he translate those particular five poems of mine for the *Gazette de Zürich?* Interesting, i.e. turbulent, but perhaps without real strength. No doubt I offer an Openness where Paul sees himself. A credible—different—Open: authentication of poetry:
—You like Rilke?
—Like Rilke! The Open…
—Yes, the Open… he concludes.

There is a trap. There is a trap between Paul and me. And the trap seems to be alternating and necessarily repetitive (What did Gisèle tell you? You've seen Gisèle, haven't you? Call her! Go see her!), between Paul, me and Gisèle. I am aware of putting myself between him and her, and aware of my power to shift the trap.

[…]

I see again his burial. I imagine his body in the coffin. He sees. Our eyes. Her eyes—in tears. Her nose, in the car, straight, slim, outlined against the air. She gives off, wears a scent. And him always there. He is watching. Watching. My gums are bleeding. Nothing will stop. Of course. He is watching. Passion in tears, moist lips.

I would like to oppose, no, juxtapose, no, posit apprenticeship and writing.

I say no. That's not the problem. Of course we have to learn, but learn orality (after Paula) at the expense (I insist) of poetry.
What is it (poetry)? And what is it in the arms of X. or Greta? A bomb, no?

Something (in words) is a prayer. Often. No, not prayer but spoken: *parole*. An oral spirituality or flash, star, flare.

Metaphor—but real. Lived.

I see again Greta walking in front of me in the snow, in Vienna, and between us we happily carry the Christmas tree.

Paul was there.

Greta.

The child, a Christmas tree with candles, snow, silver balls, angel hair—and us.

Greta in boots. Knotty knees and knotty, but vertiginous sex. On the edge of the bed. Red legs.

How to love, and then, how to talk? I mean, we slide: space allots us a word. Our roles seem more complicated for being masked.

I come to this (terrible and unarticulated) perception while translating, first by myself then beside him, "Engführung."

I translate by myself (without understanding all) "Engführung." Why this poem? Why did he request this one? He seems to offer me deciphering a possible ars poetica for the end of time. Mother carries the child. The whitewashed arches form a white moon. I am crying. The child's ear is bleeding.

Again the elder trees. Again the bleeding gums. Red. And red blood.

In the shade of the walnut tree, as a child. Deep in the garden. I know I was waiting.

The dream. The hand in the dream. The water in the dream. The bedroom in the dream. I mean: I know I was waiting for what the adult will forget.

The royal move:
—Poetry, Jean Daive, poetry!

One evening on Boulevard Saint-Michel, some years after Paul's death, Joerg Ortner turns the pages of a book he has found. He shows me the grandiose places where Rilke had lived. The relation between the poet and his space is everything. In fact, the poet writes. He is a straw in the black fever of the room he occupies.

Paul, the nightowl.

What does he do at midnight in Rue Tournefort, at the back of that buzzing courtyard?

One day I dropped a spoon in this courtyard of Rue Tournefort: the echo of its fall still sounds in my ears. A loud crash. Persistent vibrations from those walls.

He is sensitive to red threads, to designation. I designated him, sent him the manuscript of *Décimale blanche*. He did not respond. All these years (1965-1970) seemed an eternity fusing psalms and splashing rain.

The Contrescarpe is the place that welcomes the young poet. ("I salute the paulownias.") Paris, that is, the Contrescarpe.

The air tastes of dust and the ear picks up wind rustling in the leaves of our chestnut trees. We have taken refuge behind the trunks I am counting. We talk. He talks:
—Use the colon. It syncopates.
—There's not just the colon for saving...
—...saving?
—...the meaning, for example.
—Give me an example.
—I take as example: "*Einmal, /da hörte ich ihn...*"[10] you see?
—I see...
—Put a colon before the second line: you'll save a "there."
—So a colon for *da*.
—A colon for *da*.
—Fine... But for "*vernichtet, /ichten*" (*gedicht and genicht*), for example. You would put a colon for...
—No colon...You have to translate.
—And when you don't have to translate you put a colon...
Paul smiles. And continues:
—It is not always possible to shift the colon in the meaning.
—I'm glad to hear you say it.

—For *vernichtet,*/*ichten,* I suggest for example: *anéanti, néanti.*
Again he smiles. Our tensions—and we are tense—are slight.
He looks at the chestnut trees. I smile at him. My count
is thrown off. We've come to a halt. He stopped in order
to talk to me. Face to face. This stopping exasperates me.
Because it's a marker. And I don't overly like marked—*traveling*—conversations. (I have experienced them with Alain
Veinstein, CRJ,[11] and Ortner who managed to keep me
standing for 180 minutes = 3 long hours of telling me the
history of the wall and fresco in the Luxembourg Garden),
standing still in the shifting dust with smells changing from
one moment to the next. And I imagine colors, too, with
the conversation.
"We must wash Rimbaud's heart." (Joerg Ortner)

Elements of destruction, of the city destroyed during May 68.
Gun-fire. Gas. Bombs. Paving stones. Burned cars. Helmets.
Barricades. Trees knocked down.
   —This isn't the moment to rewatch *Battleship Potemkin…*
says Paul.
   —"They" would not understand your sense of humor.

We are leaving the École and turn to the right.

Sometimes his presence and our conversation echo like an
aquarium or hothouse. We feel suddenly stifled. He knows
all the plants. And later in the night, G. knows all about the
sexuality of fish.

   It is raining. The mirrors are shrouded. Who is the dead
sister?
   —I am going to see an aunt in London, he says.

Salty saliva.

When he shakes my hand he must sense an obscure grief in me and a child's stammer.

He wants to calm, veil, explain, whereas I know his darkness.

The first seconds are flashing fire, extremely fast.

Then the torment turns, the pain slides off. We can talk to each other.
— So?...
—You brought me your poems?
—Bah...
—Show them to me!
—You know...
—Yes, I know... We'll go eat at La Chope afterwards.

One afternoon he lets me read "*Du liegst im grossen Gelausche.*"[12] He explains the sieve and the sow. The murders. Rosa Luxemburg. The Eden hotel.

He evokes Berlin. His voice warm and as if muted. It no longer sounds the universe. The man turns into a child who, suddenly among ruins, does not understand the ruin of wars.
—And I have written this poem... right?...

He speaks to me at length about the murder of Rosa Luxemburg and Karl Liebknecht, with the same intensity as when he speaks of his parents shot in the concentration camp.

Orgasm and full moon. Shortly after, dinner downstairs. White tablecloth. Lit candles.

—There is no dessert tonight.
—But there never was…

The salon of the big house is white, the Aegean sea, blue. From my armchair I watch the configurations of the light against the sky. Not quite labyrinthine. The mind does not multiply. The mind does no damage. But I am drifting off. If I threw a stone I would become a wound. No… because, to reach the depth, sensitive eyes see nine methods to compose a wound differently.

I look at the sea and at the rambler behind me, its red roses. I look at the sea turned granite by the wind. The wind is blowing.

The sepulchre is open, the palm tree is open, the meadow is open. A man is digging. The stone wall reaches all the way up to the sanctuary.

The donkey motionless in the meadow's memory does not disturb the end of time.

Before me the open sea, and my thinking slowly opens up a crack. I do not want to fall from the sky. I do not want to fall into the deep. I am not a stone. I am only a wound. The chair and the rambler protect me.

In the cool of the white salon I wonder if there is a rite of passage and if Paul Celan's plunge into the Seine has the sense of crossing a threshold. It's because heaven is no longer open to man that man plunges into the waters and digs into the earth. Here too different methods compose a different vanishing.

The deep is open.

One whole summer long I look at a donkey standing in his meadow. The meadow by the sea. The motionless donkey looks out, and I think he looks beyond time at a kind of stupor that suggests sainthood.

The meadow is at the end of the village, at the end of the island. Up against the sea. The donkey seems to be waiting. Humility is certainly a threshold or an absolute dissolution whose space remains to be occupied and experienced. Together with the meadow, the sea, and the trees, the world of things assembles a geometric architecture. Time is no longer added to anything.

Neither to time nor to warm chestnuts.

In Rue de Longchamp, I look at the bookcase Paul left behind.

One day I talk to him about his library left in Rue de Longchamp.
—Yes, I miss it. I feel deprived, have deprived myself of it. You know, I had found *Le Grand Jeu* at a bouquinist's for nothing. I'll give it to you. I'll tell Gisèle to give it to you. I have found marvels... Paul Eluard, Baudelaire, Tzara, Picabia...

Gisèle makes me a present of the 1948 Vienna edition of Celan's *Der Sand aus den Urnen,* a book in three parts. The second part has always puzzled me:
"Mohn und Gedächtnis," as if memory were not captive to some poppy of the spirit.
Green branches and paved street. Gently, the humidity forms beads. Hands behind his back, thoughtful. Head bowed. He can silence the lament even if we are its backbone.

I once saw him threatening. His body threatened me. He advanced into my breathing space. I held his eye. He suddenly changed: became trusting, understanding. All in the space of a millisecond. I was trembling.

—You like ties? You change them often, Jean Daive?

—I like ties, but you don't seem to appreciate mine today.

—You know...

—Yes... I saw the way you looked at it...

—Forget it, please.

He solemnly casts down his eyes. He is pure humility. I love seeing him feel compunction. He is getting disturbed. His sadness deepens, but patience wins out. He sits down, touches his forehead, then plays with a pencil. Dejected. Looks at the telephone.

—How about going to eat by the Contrescarpe...

—Yes, let's walk, Paul Celan.

The Contrescarpe: a brownish stone garden in the dusk. A faceless sleeper at our feet, and a bit farther off clochards building a fire to heat an open tin. Black steps for a woman who enters into a façade.

The shop windows seem to reflect sad dreams. He walks and makes elusive phantom signs. Conversation is impossible. On the other hand, we make no noise.

—Come with me as far as my place.

He licks his lips. Voices fuse. He looks at fruit: sombre question.

—I won't ask you to come up. My cleaning woman... So long, Jean Daive.

He goes in.

Stark silence. Evening.

A Sunday in winter. It is snowing. I have just crossed the Seine and see Paul a ways off, in his big gray coat, crossing diagonally the Place du Palais-Royal. A certain distance, a snowy space between us. Encounter abandoned in the snow. I turn around. He is in the middle of the empty crossroad. The place is deserted and I clearly see the tracks of two paths. I turn again. He has disappeared.

I walk along the garden of the Palais-Royal. Branches covered with rime and glitter. An emptiness given shape by columns, pillars, balconies. In my mailbox I find a letter from Paul.
—I am the meridian, he told me one day.

Letter of snow. Letter of Absence. Letter of the missed encounter. Behind us today's snow and the white Seine.

Why? I don't want to look anymore. I don't get the tone. The word no longer has tone. How would you say? How would you understand?
—The secret is in these leaves. The secret is perhaps within us, he says to me. But we cannot understand all. The world is empty. The sky is empty.

I remember the small book I found in a bookstore in Hamburg, *Der Meridian:*[13]
"Ladies and Gentlemen,"
"Art, you will remember…"

Fascinated by the book and its text, its vocabulary: the

marionette, the tropes... Associating writing and the meridian, words and the meridian.

One day, a beautiful woman in a long black dress and a black quasi pirate hat looks at me and approaches:
—I'd like to talk to you... Actually, I'd like you to talk to me.
I open my mouth, and no sound comes out into our space, hers and mine.
So she anticipates, mischievously:
—If you talked to me I would not lose my true north...
—Ah.
—You know why?
—No.
—I'm a geographer.

My penis hurts tonight. Real, violent pain. As if a golf club had fallen on it. A golden club with all its weight fallen on my penis.

I would like to tell of the gold of clubs and genitals. Almost impossible. Christmas again. Paul is dead. I spend the holidays in Vienna with Greta. The green and white fir. My penis burning, bandaged. Greta smiles, always ironical: "You always dramatize everything," but suffers: her vulva is burning too. She calls emergency. No doctors available. I call Paris:
—My penis is bleeding.

Greta has bitten too deeply with a gold tooth. Nubian gold, here in a mouth (not hand).
One day I go into the Sorbonne to look at the fake frescos and the empty Great Amphitheater. Paul had the experience

of being an exhibition in a similar hall. It must have been a horror.

Gisèle tells me the horror. The fit of dementia. The neighbors' testimony. The police car. The police station. And Paul exhibited in an amphitheater to medical students who take notes.

Sun. Paul invites me to La Coupole, which he loves. Everything's red. I sit on his right.

Red benches for two men in gray. Four tables away, Philippe Sollers.

I've often walked with Joerg along the Seine at night. Paul with us in spirit, and his kind of questioning: the reflections on the still water must be the despair of surveyors. Because the Seine flows, and the glistening follows our movement. We walk, and the glitter moves toward us. Joerg was never short on frenzy.

In a café, Paul Celan goes through his identity for me in a neutral, toneless voice, the acoustic equivalent of a photomat.
—Jean Daive, I was born in Bukovina, in Czernowitz.

He weighs his words carefully. Every moment he evaluates the word. I should add: every moment he evaluates silence.

I've come to understand that a silence—is—the negative of a moment of thought and that it needs to be heard thoroughly. The moments he tells of his identity have echoes of an epic. Everything falls into place: the father, the mother, Judaism, languages, disappearances, the dismembered family regrouped in the camps, then destroyed, the war, poetry. Tours, Paris. Neutral voice, always. Nothing too much.

Time looks on. We are trembling. There must be a wound inside words that communicates. Paul Celan:
—I have paid. I can say that I have paid.

He again speaks of the German misconceptions at his expense: "Death Fugue" foremost among them. He is visibly irritated by what he tells me, and the conclusion is not long in coming.
—If there is a paradise I will certainly get there.

He gives me a quick look, but avoids my eyes. His mottled forehead gently comes near my face: he looks at me steadily, with large eyes.
—I shall translate *Décimale blanche.*
—Ah.
—I feel it will be possible... some day... But things are not always possible.

Impeccable gray-black suit. White shirt. Tie. Heavy walking shoes. He is sitting on his chair. He looks at me. He turns his tongue in his mouth. A moment of suspense and, above all, illusion. As talking is impossible for us today he makes me understand in silence, in the negative. He lets veils comes between us. I notice a big book open in a low bookcase.
—Yes, I'm reading Meister Eckhart. Look.

He shows me pages of the book. His voice, an orphan's.

He is going to come out of hospital. He tells me to meet him at the Balzar. I show I am astonished.

—Yes, at the Balzar.

—Ah.

—For the coffee pots that are so impressive…

—I go there mostly for the soup bowls… You've noticed them?

He laughs. We go on to other things.

By his side, I feel enclosed in a dark knowing without unease, without irritation. He is aware of it: no stranger to anything in the world.

A world as in a dream, nocturnal, unraveling around the paulownias of the Contrescarpe. Crates stained with peach juice, crates full of half rotten tomatoes, black hands eating almost liquid pears and bluish hearts of lettuce. He looks on.

—What one should respect, what one should not respect. It takes moderation. It takes knowing.

Some leaves turned toward the sky turn blue in the sun, cast shadows. He takes my arm and pushes me away from the rotting vegetable heap.

We walk down Rue Mouffetard.

—Moderation is never obscure, and excess is always captive of knowing. You understand?… You write the word *énoncé*. My poem denounces the world or, more exactly, announces a world to *énoncer* o-ther-wise. I am the *énoncé*, right…

He is violent. He turns shy. We're approaching the Public Baths, and the air of the Street of the "Patriarchs" calms him. His head is down. He walks. I walk.

—I write the word *coeur*. The heart, because there is no blood on us.

The clouds scatter in the distant sky and beyond the sky.
—There are two worlds: the world and the world of the star. And I haven't yet mentioned the world of the shoelace.

The water at our feet is gleaming without flashes. Children crying behind the closing gates. The water turning black like the trees. It was a beautiful day at the Luxembourg.

[...]

It is a time of wounds, of silence, of autumn. He has left the hospital. He invites me for a drink. Sun. We sit outside.
—What will you have, Jean Daive? I feel like ordering... that red drink... red... Campari with seltzer. It feels as if the palm trees of Luganowere coming to me... palms and pink drink... And you?
—Something white, green, yellow... a Lemon Perrier.

We watch the crowd of the Rue de Condé and the Rue de l'Odéon come and go. He drinks, really savoring. The pink liquid is a sensual, beatific dream.
—Patience under a gray sky. How far?... Jean Daive. How far?...

The sky is clouding over. He gets up. Shakes my hand.
—Come see me Saturday. Can you work this Sunday? We'll spend the afternoon together. I'd like to read "Und mit dem Buch aus Tarussa"[14] with you.
He takes my arm and pushes me into the Rue de l'Odéon, toward the Luxembourg.

—I once received a strange parcel addressed to me in Cyrillic script. As I took it I knew it would play a great role in my life. The parcel came from the USSR. It contained books and an anthology. A road opened for translating Mandelstam and others. Come Saturday and Sunday. We'll read "Tarussa" together.

One day Paul says to me:
—In May 68, you remember, we were all German Jews, and according to Marina Tsvetaeva all poets are Jews, right... Now I'll translate for you what she meant: all poets are Jews... contaminated...

The Contrescarpe is our dune, green with large paulownia leaves. We simply walk there. Walk across it. Simply circle it. No, its outskirts mean danger to us, a threat. It's where fear is and its street names: Rue du Pot-de-Fer, Rue Tournefort. Often we are overcome by weariness. A door closes. I walk back down the dune.

The prayer, for it is a prayer, our murmur that continues, ecstatic, in the street. Our murmur remains internal. Only a few syllables escape.
—Bah!
—Ah.

This goes with the impeccable, incorruptible character of his being. His ironed handkerchief: white square, perfect square, square without fold. Square folded and without fold. You understand?
—No, there is nothing to understand. There is the task to be and to reshape the word, i.e. a matter of memory. I already told you: the ancient murmur in the child's ear. The word in memory has something fat about it, greasy...

—A pat of butter?

—Watch out for the knifeblade…

—Yes…

The fence of the Luxembourg garden seems to observe us, and behind it, the trees, one by one, like organ pipes.

—I've thought much about the spoken word and its trace in us that I would call its drift. This drift inside us. A word heard, is that still a word, simply a word…

—I cannot answer you today, Paul Celan. I am certain, but have no way to prove it, that there is invisible work impinging on our thought which, by its nature, cannot help giving in. Giving in is not the right word…

—Thought cannot, by its nature, help thinking itself there…

—Hello, fence.

He looks at me, and together we look at the fence of the Luxembourg.

—That's where you want to see a language?

—Perhaps…

—Don't forget the human being, Jean Daive.

—Who says I do?

—I mean the human being, the Other. I already told you: it's madness. You with your love of mountains, that's one of them—one that grows along with our words, our climb. I am witness to this, and victim.

—Victim?

—Victim. Some day I'll tell you. But haven't you seen me in hospital?

The toy sailboats on the bit of water farther off turn also with Paul's phrases, vehement, dejected, ravaged. His hands are beautiful, gentle. On his forehead too, a terrible gentleness. And we walk on.

There were never any crossroads on our walks, no halts I mean, exactly as if our promenade were part of a long ribbon without beginning or end, without collision and almost without witness.

On the paving stones his step turns gentle: pure sound, muted sighs. The leaves are still and the air holds back all the doors of the silent École.
—What do you want to open, Jean Daive?

I stare at him. He senses my confusion. We are stammering. I push him toward it in spite of myself. Too late.

I like walking in the scent of blooming linden after the rain that fills the ear with warm sounds, noises, diffuse sights or, more precisely, fleeting thoughts.
—Write. Don't doubt, I mean: do not deny poetry.
—That's not easy.
—I know.
—It is not easy to find words again, I mean to relearn words or relearn to speak. It's a little as if you were coming to after seventeen years in a coma and you heard yourself pronounce one single word: "write," without any idea what that word means.

Gravely he stops and turns toward me:
—What has happened?

His voice extremely gentle. And impossible to add to, reply to—a speed, a pain behind my eyes make me dizzy. We walk on.

The crowd of cold eyes scatters. The leaves, the trees, a lit window, a woman in front of a door all take on an almost mythical charge. I ask myself today if the worry about communicating is not of the vegetal order. Man can talk and move only under the sign of the vegetable realm, hence of a millenary order of knowledge.

I am juxtaposing two moments. In the brownish garden of the École Normale Supérieure guarded by busts he likes to eye:

—Look at these stone busts, look at eternity: they are here forever...

Watching the goldfish in the pond and the bare branches, Paul develops the Goethean idea that the seed is a modified leaf.

Back from London, Paul shows me in his office a postcard of Géricault's horse struck by lightning: the horse is peaceful, and lightning strikes.

—A poet is one who touches lightning: he knows it can strike from two meters away.

—According to you, energy is a structure and develops according to numbers... And according to you eternity is a grid, the grid of the human.

—You are lending me a ladder here, Jean Daive...

We smile. We talk under the black lamps of the garden. We do not leave the École.

[...]

All summer long I look at a donkey upright against the sky. The meadow is by the sea, and the donkey stands stock-still in the abundant light. In spite of the gritty stuff of things everything seems translucid except for a gray splotch that I sometime identify as a bit of cloth or piece of bread: the donkey stares and I sense his moving off.

A storm rages. The whole island is nothing but gusts and waves of sand on the ground. The wind strong. The noise deafening. Things rise up, open, come apart. Branches break. Squalls of water shatter windows. Waves detach from the sea, fly over the meadow and hit the roofs of houses. The donkey stands stockstill. His eyes have fallen shut. I stare at him.

I run into Gisèle: "How was he? Calm? Depressed?..." I tell her a little according to a selective grid. Above all I'm aware of tracing a diagonal across shadows that form chords as in a sonata.

What I call the Aegean Sea is perhaps a displacement of the Contrescarpe. My island, a place that induces rituals or itineraries: I take cold showers with a watering hose in front of the rambler rose, I pick up nails the carpenter left on the beach, I climb up to the sanctuary, I look into the cool white hotel lobby twice a day, morning and evening, I walk a path lined with giant cactus and fig trees: to go beyond, but without thinking about the space beyond.

My rambler climbs with a passion, and I watch it climbing. The three armchairs in the lobby are covered with white sheets, and I look at this phantom garment that I sense, but do not see.

Do I follow? Do I resist? There is no answer. Or: "To inoculate is the foremost simplicity," Paul says to me in his office in Rue d'Ulm.
"Inoculate…"

I pass the night with X. Her arms never relax. We whisper. I do not look at her face. A candle is burning, throws light on her bare back. The bread and the plates, the knives and forks budge in the dark, and the shadows on the wall tremble. I tremble in her arms. Dawn light. I leave.

Chestnuts bounce, roll at our feet: nature drops out of autumn. Mild wind.
—One has to go through life with a rasp, he says.

The falling chestnuts hit the ground with a dry sound. Detonations. Nature massed in the air turns over and rolls like bursts of a meteor.
—So it is possible that the earth delimits the infinite of language…
After a long silence punctured with noise, he continues:
—The world is of glass.
—And disappearance is within us.

A woman is waiting behind walls. She eats apples and, stretched out like Olympia, reads books of Austrian thought, taking notes. She reads lying down or sometimes sitting, an always hot kettle on the floor beside her slippers. She bends down, lets her long hair fall over her face and brushes it back nonchalantly without letting go of her book and her reading. It is snowing. I bring the snow in with me, the growling of the world and a very controlled rage:
—No sooner do you come in than my tea is cold!

It is snowing. My footbridge is white, as are the roofs. I breathe the weather.

I go out into the snow, and the sides of beef that redden the butcher shops in Rue Coquillière remind me of this remark Paul made while staring at the pond of the École Normale:
—Autobiography is a goldfish...

I walk through the jumble of vegetables on the snowy ground.

This afternoon the light is blue and the air silvers the streets. A drumroll sounds in the distance, we rush toward it and, at the angle of Rue Jacob, under the four paulownias of Place Furstenberg, discover gypsies with tambourines, a ladder and a monkey in red pants. Paul remains fascinated all through the spectacle. The tame monkey wears short red pants, green suspenders and round his neck a scarf with little red dots on white. The monkey laughs, talks, thinks, and the drumrolls set the rhythm of his double somersaults.

The crowd applauds. Paul smiles. He reconnects with an ancient joy.
—The East is coming all the way to us.

He seems really joyous. Delighted by the sound of the tambourine.
—Don't you think that a drum is a bit like a mother's heart?

The giant leaves of the paulownias recall the size of the monkey's ears.

His gaze joins the universe, decomposing its memory and perhaps its reflections. His gaze joins a theater, not all of whose storms he can master, nor all its bridges, as if the places now (one after the other) broke loose, drifted off (one after the other) without him, without us, and severed us from the real paths: the hospital, Rue Tournefort, Rue d'Ulm, the clinic, Rue de Longchamp.

—Passage still takes place in language. That's all I have left. But how much longer? There are no more real bridges, right... The poem has burned them all. I shall accept Gisèle's proposal. I shall accept moving to Avenue Emile-Zola. I need to pitch my tent.

Again snow and cold. Again the huge branches of the chestnut trees with us walking underneath. A street vendor sells warm chestnuts, and Paul smiles:

—The East drawn by the warm chestnuts is here to sell them to us, and it is the unengendered offspring that peels them... I'll get some, we can eat them while walking.

I remember the feel of our breath and our mouths biting in the cold.

Again chestnuts roll all around us and here and there burst open. Drift carries off the rolling chestnuts, and each one is a god without a bridge. Rolling gods: Yahweh, Christ, Moses, the Self. The bridges are burned.

—I'll teach you how to peel a chestnut.

The gods are already peeled. Appealed to and peeled. The gods roll. They have no trees. They fall. They roll. We roll. The gods.

We both live in an attic. I can imagine bridges from the skylight to the gods. Twilight and light. The hills (the attic and the gods) communicate. We walk. It's a dream. I wake up.

I have not seen him read. Or seldom.

He walks. He turns. The page. The world. Us. He returns books.

I have not seen him write. Or seldom. Once, for a long time. Twice. Three times. No, four. Rather often after all, I think.

Our rendez-vous is at the École Normale. It is evening. Nobody there. Night falls. The empty hallway echoes, vibrates. In the distance, voices. I wait. An hour. An hour and a half. Two hours. The brownish garden gets dark and disintegrates into large shadows. The stone eternities do not separate anything. In their niches.

The day after, a letter from Paul. Held up at the clinic, he writes.

[...]

We look at the walls. We read the walls. A May of blossoming trees. A May of goldfish. Paul watches, fascinated, a billsticker. We read Artaud on the walls. We read: The One Alone exists. And his voice reads to me what's written on the walls. He says:
—Our mirrors of today are the walls.

The stars have set. The pink crowd of dawn. I'm writing on the toilet.

A melody of yellowed leaves accompanies us and interleaves our silences, which he knows to keep, provoke, appease. Anxiety darkens his face, and his silence tries to stave off fright. His arms end in hands he keeps clenched. He will remain mute, my lips painfully dry. But the ear follows the cries of a little girl at grips with an imaginary game.

Very softly he hums, his mouth closed, while looking at the posters on the fences or hurriedly glued on tree trunks: spots of color, shiny on the skin of the air. We move along these manifestations of civic anger, his hands behind his back, mine in my pockets. The sun is shining, and flashes of gold sweep over the facades.

A woman is sweeping the street. Her heap of leaves and dust grows visibly. Her movements almost symptomatic of age-old knowhow: with an incredibly light touch that makes her broom literally fly, she describes the figure eight that she doubles and repeats to the infinite: an infinite eight bound and closely watched, like most of our walks.

—It's beautiful the way her dress swings around her legs, and the broom moves without pause. She'll stop only when she runs out of dust...

—... or leaves...

—... or leaves... yes... Do you think that for lack of dust she could allot this motion to a madness whose mental object would correspond to the broom, for example?

—...

—... I often watch the street sweeper. He has changed, and his broom does not recognize him.

—It too has changed.

—The broom has changed, and the sweeper has lost the gesture that reproduces in real time the sign of the infinite, which is that of the Open.

—...

—I have often watched the drains and the dreams that wash down the drains, silvery, and in this running puddle have often imagined an absolute sweeper, master of the perfect gesture, able to tamp down the dust of the whole world.

—The dust comes back… the song comes back… What does not come back?

—A woman won't come back!

—And as for the word, you know?…

—Sometimes, I know, I know it will come back…

He looks at his wedding band and turns it on his finger. Gold— amid children's cries and flashes of sun.

—Let's go eat at La Chope, I'll invite you.

Paul orders two steaks and two glasses of port that stay with us all through lunch. The two plates arrive, followed by the two glasses of port. Paul looks at me, smiling:

—I won't say, to the health of the serpent.

We raise our glasses and drink. The blue air above us is still forming a vault that shelters the Contrescarpe.

—All things considered, this place is safe, protected. I often spend my days here on the hill without getting off it.

—Coming to see you I crossed a fence with an empty lot behind it. Clochards were sleeping there. I think they recognized me. They were part of the gang tossing empty wine bottles the other night… you remember…

—I remember perfectly…

—…but what fascinated me: in walking toward them I was sinking into the ground, and it was sand…

—Ah! always the beach under our feet, underneath us…

—Your hill is sandy…

—Yes, and sand doesn't make the best pillow for my nights.

He seemed to grow slightly dejected as he said this. A long silence followed. The noise of the square penetrated into the café. We finished our lunch.

After her return from the morgue, Gisèle described his corpse tome: "Paul was black. His head was all black." And I immediately visualized "the Savior's dark head platted in thorns," for his presence always had the feel of a person possessed by intense spirituality. This presence of the spiritual determines the poetic emulsion according to the quality of attributes, images, lives, readings, the moment of memory, information, news, the day, in short all the chance happenings that it generates and sorts out.

He sorts. Always. He tears up. I've surprised him in his office sorting letters and papers with feverish exasperation. He sorts. He tears up letters, papers with extraordinary violence, other sheets, flyers, advertisements with rage, passion, fury, despair, revolt. His waste basket always overflows with paper torn, but not crumpled into balls as with others I know.

A voice is a mask, and talking does not mean saying. Walking back down the hill I often surprise myself having a different voice or, rather, finding myself without any. I enter into another memory of which I know—practically—nothing. The word practically may elicit a smile. For what has practice to do with the memory of another man whose reflection so deeply interiorizes all the images around him. Paul has set up a caution between us: silence as reverberation of our interiority. He understands my perturbations, and I his.
    —You know... (very long silence)... Ingeborg Bachmann... (what is he getting at?)... (very long silence)... (his voice

deliberate, thick, above all deliberate, and very distant)... (does he want to tell me a fable... the East... or?)...

—I've read some poems by her...

—They aren't always very good... (very long silence)... We knew each other... she expected much from me... in life... and I disappointed her very much... but I loved her... then I met Gisèle...

—Yes...

We are ambling along the Avenue des Gobelins. He speaks slowly. A real prayer. His voice solemn. I feel his memory in vertigo, but every word is chosen with mature consideration. I feel the dense silence does not hamper what he wants to tell me.

—This was long ago... right...

—You are thinking of the Group 47...[15]

—Yes... which I knew also...

His right hand sweeps the air. It's time, he seems to signal, to have done with all this, "right"...

—Yes, Jean Daive... let's have done with all this... right? Let's meet next Saturday.

A pattern of moss and grass. A pattern of tufts between paving stones, an uninterrupted line at our feet, line of writing or line of promise or line of torment that leads us beyond ourselves. Leaves us behind. Precedes us.

—This line of grass anticipates us, Jean Daive... Take note.

It follows us. Intersects with us.

I imagine his black skull covered with grass... I see this black head in black-and-white and Gisèle's tears, in black-and-white.

The beyond in the offing and deliverance, no doubt in black-and-white. Deliverance.

Uninterrupted line that crosses and divides us, line of writing that anticipates our end. End of Paul Celan in Paris, in the Seine. End of Ingeborg Bachmann three years later, in Rome, found burned to death in her bed. How?

"Paul had to die so that we could meet in the word *énoncé*," Joerg Ortner said to me one day in the pink streets of Florence. "You realize, Jean, that we first met on the Place des Vosges to talk about the word *énoncé* that Paul could not translate. It is incredible."

Perhaps Paul did not want to translate it, and that is the best he could do for the two of us (Paul and me): to leave the last word for the end, and the end here is the *énoncé* of death... the declaration... without subtitle, Joerg, the terms of death, but not subtitled...

There is a symptom of Paul's I would like to analyze, that of avoidance. But I wonder if the reader has not perceived its structure, perhaps its grid and frequency all along our meetings, our walks.
I hear him say to me:
—The thorn is not what you think, I don't mean spine, not this hill.[16]
—The thorn has no crown...
—No, not a crown of thorns. The man of today wears a hat.

Remember that portrait of Kafka with his hat at an angle? There the thorn would rather be in the eye, in the fire of the eye.

—What are you getting at?

—The heart bleeds because of the thorn... the thorn in the side of the man awake without recourse or sleep... The Camp is the thorn. Memory is the thorn... also the sun...

He is shivering. Trembling. I walk across his barely lit office. The dense night in the garden of the École Normale breaks against the windows. We sit down. He stares fixedly at his desk. Fixedly. His hands on his desk. Dejected. He no longer knows I am near him, with him. He raises his head and says:

—Jean Daive.

We say goodbye. I disappear. Walk back down the hill whose thorny spine he is.

This hill without a tree, this "peeled" hill he loves. He leaves it only rarely, for necessary expeditions.

Sometimes air touches his hands. Hands that sometimes, like today, look peeled. White and "peeled." Burned. Peeled as after a burn.

Peals, fading peals of a bell above the hill. I am suddenly afraid. Gripped by apprehension. I enter his office. He is somber, menacing. We leave immediately. The Contrescarpe. La Chope. He says:

—You don't need silverware to approach a bug.

—It isn't eaten.

—Too flat for that... One doesn't need knife or fork because it is invisible, eternal and invisible...

—That's a lot of attributes...

—It has two and they are unclassifiable... I mean... these two attributes make thinking of it unclassifiable.

—So it exists and man does not see it.

—Or else: it does not exist, it is invisible and man declares it...

—There is a link between the bug that is invisible and the Contrescarpe.

—That would make it the counterscarped bug... if you like.

Peals, fading peals of a bell above the hill. Faint.

Rain, drumming on the leaf-covered glass. The wind whips up the rain, almost up to the open window. It is morning, as today is morning for yesterday... right... Time breaks through. Time hangs over us, and its duration opens onto moments of past words. Today's rain falls on yesterday. Steps come back. I am very hungry. Very thirsty. Very afraid. Along a passage that allows me to see stars shining at night and roofs gleaming brightly during the day. Along a passage whose space becomes that of the wanderer on earth. Rain falls outside the warm room.

—I have hidden the blood. My poems hide the blood. What do you think? I have paid... I have paid, he says.

Rain stings the air, hits the silvery window panes. Today for yesterday. Today for words said earlier whose structure was perhaps not yet thought out...

Peals, fading peals of a bell above the hill, above the funeral procession rolling over the sand. Sandy Paul with a black head, and there already, visible above the crowd, the black hat of his friend.

—I have hidden the madness... My poetry masks the madness.

Driving through Düsseldorf with Konrad Klapheck in 1985, we pass a fake Greek temple with columns: "Paul Celan has read here!"

I often pass the day among the animals of the Jardin des Plantes, walk among the wild beasts and stare for hours at an eagle in his cage: the one that I watch and superimpose on Paul's, caught in an interleaved tale: Paul's eagle chews on a shoelace (the infinite) come loose from the world.

Watching Paul Celan eat I always thought his jaw was *holy.*

Nobody reads any more. Nobody comes any more.
—I have read you attentively. I have read *Decimale blanche* and loved its impalpable concrete-abstract nature. The tale is merciless, familiarly merciless. You know what I mean... The structure is perhaps that of a chessboard. The corridors, the flagstones, the black and white. The mother and what is not the mother. There is a sense of watching, the thing observed is under surveillance, isn't it... Nobody ever talks of the methods of watching. I am thinking of watching observed from inside language and of its effects on the reader... Ah... there is of course Franz Kafka... But that's not what I want to say... Watching need not necessarily lead to fable, caricature, expressionism. You know what I mean... Everything needs to be masked... even observation. Remember the first sentence of *Malte Laurids Brigge:* So I was being watched. This remains right, even for a first sentence... What is or is not said before this first sentence permits this one: The character comes from farther away than the book and goes farther... But you think I stress a watching that could come to us only in prose... The prose of vigil and watch... A beautiful text in perspective... To cut out observation seems difficult, rare... I often think of a watching whose absolute locus would be the keyhole: the hole as the measure of all surveillance. But to write of watching presupposes neutrality, distance, the mask that only verse can betray... Replace a dormitory or soup kitchen under

observation with a verse and you get the poem at white heat. You get incandescence, you get a haunted poem… I've seen it… I've understood it in translating "Le Bateau ivre"…Rimbaud was watching me… the poem was watching me… and verse after verse… for a long moment of unforgettable grace… I glimpsed the just betrayal that allowed me to find equivalence in terms of betrayal… Betrayal articulates almost every verse… I was jubilant… and I love this betrayal, which went completely unnoticed… Yes, your book has this density of observation—haunted observation—doesn't it… I no longer sleep. I am haunted by the reality, more and more likely, of his death. The blue sky of April days, then of May days makes memory volatile. Gisèle investigates day and night: nothing escapes her, every detail is taken into account, and told in almost epic manner (I am thinking of Paula). She anticipates drama, that is, suicide. She sets the scene and above all states her deductions: he enters his bedroom, goes to bed, he puts down his watch, he gets up, goes down the stairs, crosses the avenue, climbs over the railing of Pont Mirabeau, throws himself into the Seine.

I see Gisèle. Her tear-stained face upsets me. She weeps, but pulls herself together. There is great strength in her. Unflinching.

The day of my birthday Gisèle offers me a page torn from a notebook of Paul's. It is the page with the poem he gave me for the first issue of *fragment*. In one stroke, Paul sets down lightning, all the words seized with unheard-of speed.

The word speed reminds me of our rapid-fire exchanges (though sometimes they were the opposite: slow as in an aquarium). One day he is searching for a table and asks me how to go about it. I give him the name of a friend who might be helpful.

—I called the friend you mentioned.

—Ah... What do you think of her?

—I think she's loyal.

—Usually she is so only by chance or exception (laughs). But does she have what you are looking for?

—Not really... She has to think about it.

—Think about what you are looking for? Aren't you simply looking for a table, in fact?

—In fact? I'm looking for a table, yes... but...

—But you are not really looking for a table.

—Yes, I am looking for a table, but I couldn't really use it...

—Use will come with the table...

—Yes, that's true... so I wasn't wrong to use the word use, I mean the word loyal about your friend. You've twisted the meaning... It's her loyalty that brings up the use of the table... She needs to think about the use I'll put the table to... She asked me to call back... After a time for her and me to find the use of the table.

—Where do you want to put it, this table?

—In principle in the living room, which is fairly large and looks out on the trees and the Seine. I'll show you the apartment...

Will you come see me Avenue Emile-Zola?

—Yes.

It is at this "table," which turns out monumental, four meters long, that I discover at his side his translation of *Décimale blanche*.

I want to come back to this table and what it brings up for me. The table chosen by Paul and put in the apartment of Avenue Emile-Zola is the replica of one of the many tables in the hospital refectory, where he sat to talk to me. Same dimensions, same placement perpendicular to the window, a collective table for one single man.

There is rain among other sounds, and the steps I hear fuse with the noise of the earth. An echo of muted hissing rises up toward me. It is fall and it is raining. A leaning fall, for Paul comes from farther away than the longest wait. Why leaning? A man leaning over a leaning fall. I think of the movement of poems. I think of the movement of song. The movement of masts. Song against earth and man against earth. I see his black fingernails: the earth there also.

The table allows me to superimpose two places. The Hospital of Sainte-Geneviève-des-Bois: Paul at the end of the table, his back to the window, steering me to a chair on his left, and Avenue Emile-Zola: Paul at the end of the table, facing the window, steering me to a chair on his right. In the hospital we talk much, he is inexhaustible. He even draws my attention to it. At his place, that is, in a barely furnished apartment (there's only the table and a few chairs), we do not talk, we work on the translation of *Décimale blanche*. So around one object there is repetition of the same and repetition of its reversal. The table turns. The table returns. Turns around.

Everything seems to return. A recollection:

One Saturday afternoon in the fall we are in Rue d'Ulm. I come to pick up Paul Celan at the École Normale and we walk down Boulevard Saint-Michel. At his usual kiosk he stops, and I see him buy *Die Zeit*. Walking on, he feverishly opens the newspaper, starts taking it apart, tossing the pages he does not want. The struggle against bulk continues for a long moment since this edition of the German weekly has all sorts of sections. It's an enormous, invasive, absorbing job. I have the impression that the entire crowd is looking at us, watching Paul sort, separate, toss. In the end he keeps what interests him, that is, the literary pages and puts them in his pocket. Our bus is supposed to take us close to the Opera. We cross the Seine, the Louvre, the square of the Palais-Royal, and ride up the Avenue de l'Opéra. At the Palais Garnier we get out, Paul Celan first, who is dumbfounded to discover at his feet the newspaper *Die Zeit,* complete:

—Jean Daive, the newspaper has returned to me in its entirety... You see, this happens to me with everything, every day.

One last remark about the same and its reversal. Having a name supposes a signature, for example Paul Antschel. One day, this signature turns around and becomes Paul Celan.

The air is mild, we hear echoes of a drumroll.

—That's the dancing monkey. Let's go see, Jean Daive.

We quicken our pace. I just quicken my pace; Paul Celan quickens his pace calmly and with grandeur. By and by we come to a fairground scene at the moment when the rays of the sun put a blue tinge on the purplish paulownia blossoms: a ceiling of blue air covers the imaginary stage set up in the space between the four trees of the Contrescarpe: gypsy woman with tamburine, little girl with a hoop, gypsy and drum, red step-ladder and bilboquet mounted on the top step, to which clings...

—a goat... they have replaced the monkey with a goat... he says.

—They are regressing.

—But they've tied around its neck the same kerchief with little red dots.

The goat balances on the bilboquet, immobile during the drumrolls.

—I miss the monkey... he continues... the monkey's grimaces and especially his disturbing glance. As if his mere glance already carried speech.

—You are thinking of potential speech, articulated at the level of a gesticulation of nerves and muscles.

—I am thinking of a cultural monkey that comes to us from the most remote ages and lands in a scene of our imagination: here on the Contrescarpe in the middle of the xxth century, a monkey who talks to us of stammering, dreamily seductive in his scarf with little red dots.

—The goat disappoints you?

—You know, the goat also stutters, that is, it gibbers because it bleats.

—The goat stutters?

—Yes.

—Don't you think the little red dots on white ground could visually announce the holes of the stutter?

—Syllabic holes, red on white?...

—Syllabic holes tied around the neck...

—Daring... or prophetic on the part of the monkey or goat. I'll think about this, I'll think about the fable.

He watches the goat tied to the bilboquet. He watches it climb down the step-ladder to the roll of the drum. He smiles. There is applause. A crowd in purplish light. I ask him:

—How do you, Paul Celan, get from stammer to stutter?

—The stammer is linked to childhood, the stutter to knowledge.

—If I understand correctly, your idea of stammer and stutter is close to Hölderlin's idea of ideal states...

—That is...

—Hölderlin says there are two ideals: extreme simplicity, childhood for you, and extreme knowledge, i.e. your stutter.
—Yes, the stutterer is literally dumbfounded. He is "stupid," that is to say aphasic, and we can think of Hölderlin.
—The monkey is aphasic, therefore...
—Therefore he dances... he has seen the lightning. He is silent and dances.

One winter. In La Chope. Paul orders wine and two omelets. The omelets are served.
—My omelet is burned, he says.
—Mine is not.
—Yours is not?
—Your omelet is burned. And you eat it anyway?
—Anyway! Yes, I eat an omelet that is burned.
He says this in a hollow, sombre voice.
I pursue:
—Would you like us to exchange our omelets?
—Impossible. What is burned cannot be changed or exchanged, right... It's a sign.
—And you keep the sign for yourself?
—That is to say...
—You do not want to exchange it?
—With you? (He is appalled.)
—You think this apparently ill-omened idea has something to do with incest?
—Perhaps...
—Like the monkey and the goat...
—The word *singe*, monkey, is in the word *signe*, sign...
—Like stammer and stutter...
—Perhaps... (a pause)... What are you doing afterwards?
—After...
—After the omelet.

—I'll go home.

—You'll go home?

—Yes, I'll go home.

— I'd like to come see you some day.

—?!! (I'm appalled.) You know it's a simple place, very simple, with a blanket instead of a door.

—Your door is a blanket?

—Yes, but it's an inner door.

We laugh. He will come. We fix the date.

At a glassed-in sidewalk café in Rue Soufflot:

—The ground is getting warmer and the snow melts. There is no more snow.

—You state that the way some people say: There are no more children or: There is no more poetry. Disappointment is taking over.

—No, I just said: There's no more snow, and as for the rest, I prefer not to talk about it.

—Talk about disappointment, or the rest?

—The two go together. Inseparable. Let's go.

Shortly after getting out of the hospital Paul invites me to a restaurant. He imperiously orders for both of us: two steaks and two Tuborg. This determination leaves me wondering, especially his choice of Tuborg. I watch the meeting of his dry, parched, "bald" lips with the foam that gently "hops" them.

Toward the end of winter, Paul visits me on Rue Coquillière. He crosses the footbridge and notices the three leaves carved in lead. He comes in, charmed by the place.

—Your place is a place of poetry. A poet's place.

Too taken aback to reply, I wait for him to finish his praise to announce:

93

—You know, the meal will be just as simple.

—Ah.

—Tomatoes with shrimp.

—Ah.

—Tomatoes with shrimp, the fresh shrimp have been shelled one by one by...

—Like my poetry, in short: every verse has been shelled, every word.

—Yes.

Paul seems paralyzed by what he sees: the non-charm of the place takes effect.

—It's really strange here.

Then he can't stop staring at the right angle facing him under the ceiling. He looks down, sitting in the wicker armchair (between cradle and hell) that I abandoned one night in 1984 in the street, while thinking of Paul. An hour later the chair had disappeared.

The color purple gave rise to a conversation with Paul that was strange:

—There is a particular light the paulownias have in spring when they flower, he said.

—A purplish light.

—Very sweet to the walker...

—Hence to him who looks or penetrates.

—Yes.

—This purplish light makes me think of the asparagus tips in my childhood that were also purplish.

—In your childhood?

—Yes: I watched the asparagus grow because as soon as you see the tip above the ground you must cover it with earth, day after day. The tip is rendered purplish by the air, and the stem remains white because it grows underground.

—Nature is strange, isn't it? What you tell me here is bizarre.

[...]

One freezing night I walk across Les Halles on my way back to Rue Coquillière. Among the apple crates, a man is sleeping on some red netting. I look at the sleeper's ear: a hole one could blow into.

My gums are bleeding. I am asleep, and the frozen blood wakes me. Pillow stained red. Paul stained red in my sleep, my pillow under his arm:

—It's a star.

—It's a pillow.

—Fold it like a handkerchief.

—A handkerchief with little red dots and words full of holes.

—It's the holes we have to write, Jean Daive, don't forget it.

—I already try to write and write transitively.

—Ah yes! Your transitive God that you hide up your sleeve.

—I have never hidden anything up my sleeve, neither God nor books.

—The gods don't read any more to men.

—Yes, men know it.

—That's why we read for the gods, right, and we write in order to read to the gods.

Something moves off, floats around his face, I don't look. I don't speak. He is waiting. His eyes are blank. I look for both of us, for him and for myself, but a sound breaks on the silence of the children. Paul whispers his discomfiture into my ear. My ear is covered with stamen and blood. "We must grow up," he murmures. "We must grow up." I wake up.

The village of the Contrescarpe dries in the sun and still hides old paths that stop abruptly at certain palissades. The empty lots are forgotten prayers.

—Have you ever examined the earth in an empty lot, he says: it's dirty, worn, mixed with brick, stone, tiles, moss, pieces of wood, springs, all sorts of things. A life seems to be stopped, and yet this lot is a stage.

—A stage for sleeping clochards and playing children.

—I have seen children here who imitated swaying on an imaginary boat. They rowed above dirty grass, earth full of oil puddles; above all they rowed before a world of sleepers.

—Strange the way the façade of a house becomes a palissade.

—Yes, and the way every house is reduced to the state of an empty lot seems stranger yet.

—Why? Because you think the vertical gives way to even surfaces, and speech to stammering?

—Perhaps… But what's certain is that every upright thing gives way to its horizon.

—May I interpret?

—I'm listening.

—You mean to say that a sister gives way to her horizon which is incest?

Paul stares at me, startled, and seems not to want to hear. An angel passes, and the passers-by make metal noises.

—Jean Daive, I have an appointment. Will you accompany me as far as the bus?

—Yes.

—The bus stop is… Feuillantines.

—Ah…

I am sitting on the Place de la Contrescarpe today, April 17, 1989, on Edith's right. I look at the four very young paulownias and at the clochard asleep under their leaves. I have the bizarre realization that the first letters of Greta, Olga, Gisèle form the three letters of Gog. Then who is Magog? The same clock tells the time, tells the confusion of times. How did all this start?

One winter, at the window, I watch the snow falling and, turning around, I see in the room a shadow with a foamy head: Greta, skull plunged into a basin, is washing her hair.

Some years later I distractedly stare at an inner horizon that separates me from her and, turning around, notice Olga bald, her hair in her hands.

Twenty years later, I buy a display case from a hair salon that I put Rue Coquillière. Joerg surprises me as I am setting it up and says:
—All that's lacking is the hair of *Décimale blanche*.

End of autumn. Rain. Men with spades are digging a hole that will turn into a trench. Paul Celan sees the yellow soil and a spade glistening in the rain.
—We have to leave some day because man puts off his end. His torment and his end.

Here he achieves the diction of the Savior in negative as, in death, the head of the Savior in black. He walks straight ahead on Rue des Écoles, his hands behind his back.
—You mean gold rises to the surface, Paul Celan?

—Yes, this kind of gold surfaces, like memory. Everything surfaces. Everything doubles: is double, of course, the hand and the spade, but the hole is for you and for me.

We walk up the hill. We approach a fence just as a clochard, a liter of wine in his pocket, disappears behind it:

—Don't look at those who enter. They enter your space, he says.

Paul stands before the fence: he takes on an air of extreme humility that I've sometimes spotted in his syntax, as if I didn't know what grammarian's mask used the detour of a sentence to project a feigned indifference toward the world. I talk to him of Rilke and his pathological humility likely to make grist of any disarray.

—You mean to say humility anticipates fears? No doubt. Man does not have enough human time to learn all the roles and he is surely born with this one: humility. So why try out others? You just said, make grist of, but don't forget that humility launders.

—So today you prefer the laundry to the mill.

—Yes.

Smiles. I accompany him to Rue Tournefort. There I am treated to the ritual phrase:

—Jean Daive, give me a call. I won't invite you up. My cleaning woman did not come today.

We shake hands. His smile is enigmatic. I walk back down the hill.

With Gisèle, the question of the wedding ring comes up.

Clenched hand. The ring resists.

At one end of my Greek island there is a donkey I watch. He does not move. He does not eat. He does not work. His immobility gets the better of time. The day I spend amid the still green pears of a café set back from the sea becomes a mere mass of observations. The donkey is all I think about. He augments a distance.

When I close my eyes I see again the maid asleep on a table-cloth so sumptuous it could stand for an implicit moral: the maid is found asleep in a halflight that defines no place, no object, no utensil. Her head is resting on her hand, and the table covered with an oriental cloth comes up to it, up to the edge of her sleep.

I get up at night. I stare at the moon above the meadow. The donkey stands motionless. He does not let anything encroach. What role of transition does he play?

In the solitude of the island, the donkey's presence sometimes rends the air. He cries, he weeps, he brays. I hear him. And I hear within me a still living mass fall into the sea, into the Seine.

Gisèle Celan, who has taken off her wedding ring, runs into Paul in Avenue Emile-Zola. He immediately notices that the ring is gone. A few days later I run into Paul at the Contrescarpe. His finger too is without ring.

A temple freshly whitewashed stands on top of a cliff above the Aegean Sea. The place is quiet and windy. I look down on my island. I notice the donkey in his meadow, the flower garden where I sit and read, the café tables under the pear trees, all the vegetable gardens, and the sea.

I enter the holy place with the white, naked walls. I light a can-dle, a second, a third, and involuntarily start counting the hot chestnuts I peeled at Paul's side. There were thirteen heaped in a cone of newspaper.

I run into Gisèle. Her hand has lost its gold.

[…]

Eric Celan captivates his father with card tricks: a different kind of magic.

—Eric is a juggler… He makes cards appear: kings, knaves, queens.
—Kings, knaves, queens.

Speaking of Eric, Paul Celan used the word megaphone: to speak into a megaphone. I can imagine the scene.

Childhood has a refuge in winter, which for us would be made of paulownia wood. All it would take is a whistle, some marbles, and we'd think we are in short pants. Paul is cheerful, smiling:
—How old are you, Jean Daive?
—Twenty-five.
—Ah.
—And you have already written *Décimal blanche*.
—Mmmm…
—Did you write something else before?
—No. Nothing before.
My no is firm, decisive. Paul understands:
—Did I offend you by asking that?
—No, but I don't understand what it is supposed to mean…
—You think it is supposed to mean something beside what is said about *Décimal blanche*.

—Nothing has been said about *Décimal blanche.*
—Not today, true... But you know... For your book, you know...
—Yes, and what are you driving at?
—It is interesting... for...
—My book.
—Yes... there is also a biographical interest.
—Out of which verses are supposed to be made?...
—Out of what wounds do they come?
With these words Paul sinks into thought. We walk on, then he comes back with:
—What was your home like?
—A wide street, with many trees. Wide sidewalks. A gate, a thick hedge, a small garden, a flight of steps and, finally, a door. Curiously, the house is a cube.
—So your home was already one of my dice, right, and you were inside!
—How do you interpret the presence of a garden before the steps?
—As a nicety... So life was set back?
—Hell was set back. Set back from the sidewalk.
—So, I hold on to the word nicety.
The afternoon is sunny, and the wind rocks the heavy branch of a chestnut tree as if it were a palm.
—The true branch forms an elbow in the air.
—Have you written this?
—No, I'm giving you my thought.
—Is it a thought you share with someone?
He smiles because he knows I want him to say:
—No, it's a thought that came before reading, before discovering André's line. But you interrupted me. I wanted to distinguish the true branch from the perfect branch.
—The perfect branch?

—The perfect branch forms an elbow in space and is covered with moss.

—Ah! and its chestnuts never fall...

—Or fall upward...

—...on the moss.

We walk side by side, the Seine black on our right. We step over ladders, tables, chairs, cross bridges, walk along façades, railings, more façades, walls, more walls. Two voices. We are two voices. One low, the other toneless. Many juvenile gestures. Complicit looks. Smiles. Lots of complicity. We linger under the mass of a paulownia, then make for the chestnut trees farther on. Night. Moon. We talk. Jubilantly. The *"Aufklärung."* "Hung up on the inner corpse," Paul Celan quotes Artaud. "There are two ideal states for man: extreme simplicity and extreme culture." A remembered poster: "The One Alone exists." We look down on the moist leaves. Rustlings that we interpret. We advance into the swinging night. The invisible.

—But, don't you think... the sign!

—The sign when our eyes met.

—When my eyes questioned yours, your finger was sliding along a knife blade.

—While we were being read by the Terrorist on the second floor?

—Yes: the scythe of delirium. After so many others. I know it well, the delirium of paulownia and chestnut.

—The delirium of East and North.

Laughter. Puzzlement. Roofs glide by above the trees. Play of hands. Lowered foreheads. The weight of the world. Our fears. Our statements. Our wanderings. Plenitude. Fatigue. At the edge of an undefinable end. Within a terrible struggle. Shreds of sentences and moons. Syllables lost in the night. Something wild. Something dark. Happens. "Everything happens like an internal story: memory of linen, the branch and the garden."

—Passing. Is resemblance the passing of the world, the place, abyss or death of the world? Trees resemble each other, like deliriums, rivers.
—Insistence is all.
—Insistence and nothing.
Night. Night not attained. Never. Something simple. Something penetrating. Simplicity, the night of our voices. Bitterness. A taste of copper and death. To embrace the grave and the unique, the inexhaustible and the word. Portion of the dice. Portion of Us. "My eyes. My eyes."

Moans. We mingle with the crowd, the trees. Among human beings. Distance. The unsayable. Solitude. As the basic planes.
—Passing: does it mean keeping what is destroyed?

Steps. Fatigue. Two cold mouths. Two black roots in the night. Without body. Without white shadows. Nothing shows outside us. Behind our faces our substance. Form full of blind formulas.
—And man? Watch out. You know: man turns on man.

His hands shoo off invisible presences. Struggle. Tenseness. The hostility of things. Familiar hostility and humiliating humiliation. He appeals to the law: "Let it be my witness." He displaces hallucination. The inhabited night. He inhabits all of night and the Night.

In the name of an indecipherable sign. Threatening movements. He is indeed threatened.
—I was in a hotel room in London when I saw God under my door: a ray, a streak of light.

—Sometimes: God. Sometimes: Nothing. What we insist on, what the eye adds.

—What the eye adds: oranges to the privet hedge.

—Or a vegetable to the dead.

—A vegetable added to the dead? Explain. Name it.

—The vegetable of graves.

—Have I told you that I've repeatedly found my newspaper, left at home, in front of the grave I had come to scrub and clean? Have you never been troubled by the number of newspapers left in cemeteries by people who have done with them? Note: I use leave.

—Text for the dead.

—Text and death.

—Under the sign of cleaning.

He talks. He fades out. His hands of darkness. Black hands with earth under the nails. Tired: an end or the end. But his gait is lordly, triumphant. He walks. He moves forward. Endlessly. Beyond. His hands clench, gather differences, appease the night. He talks. Again his hands. His fingers search for his pulse. He counts: "The time, the beat of falling." Endlessly.

—You know, insanity—the only insanity—does not lead to being engrossed with death. It leads to rejecting dialogue. Taking on the lightning bolts of the sky. Yes. I am talking to you, right. Taking on dread. Yes. Who is afraid? But taking on the body of what is uncommunicable. No. Dialogue, obsession with dialogue, imminence of dialogue: a madness.

Open mouth. From our open mouths only a murmur, a moan. Silent curse at a torn fingernail. Screaming: almost. A scream hypnotizes all hiding of the outcome or all marking of the outcome.

—The scream: is that what intelligence is?

He thinks: I am a scream of God. A searching growl. Vacillation. Slowness. Perplexity. Different reading.

—But a scream can burrow into wound and scar. A kind of saliva, basically, that attenuates the pain.

—I believe the scream is the chosen stance of a voice evicted from itself, mortally wounded, silent, terribly, become noninstrumental from being dispossessed, blank. A drunken voice, crouching. That regards no-one...

—A geometric scream.

On one foot, then on the other: insomniac gait. Oppression. Opaque. Obstacles. The din of perception. Night. Two trajectories. Screams. Words on parallel tracks. Night. Two meteors. The last branch, the last tree, and to return. The shadows turn, and to return. Return? Return.

—You wrote the word insistence. Keep it always. Don't share it.

The path is steep all the way up to the sanctuary above the sea. It is difficult, long, sometimes dangerous. Extremely bare. Behind me growls the Aegean. I turn around and see the trumpets of the Pont Mirabeau blow toward Avenue Emile-Zola, toward the apartment with the dark windows. This is darkest night above the sea with its stinging brightness. The wind is blowing. The path rising. Why interrupt a scene in motion?

End of summer. A warm day. We are in his office at the École Normale.

—I met Ungaretti. He invited me to lunch and gave me his book with an incredible inscription. Read it. Italians spit diamonds.

I listen. I listen above all to his jerky diction that detaches every word, almost every syllable. The words so detached plunge into a state of waiting that indefinitely prolongs my listening. Paul creates an aquarium effect that muffles what he communicates, makes it hard to hold on to, hold on to immediately.

—Have you read it?

—Why did you agree to meet him?

He looks at me. He knows that I know. His lips relax into a smile.

—What do you mean?

—Ungaretti could bring you news of Rome.

—Which means…

—Isn't he the adoptive "father," a kind of half-father, as we could say half-sister of…

He sees what I am getting at. He interrupts:

—We?

—You prefer the impersonal to the we?

—I prefer the impersonal, yes, especially for a remark whose outcome I don't know…

—Is Ungaretti not the half-father of Ingeborg Bachmann?

—And who is the other?

—Perhaps you?

He smiles.

—We could say so.

—We could say so or it is possibly true?

—You think my work is impersonal?

—It tries to be.

—A try is never a success, a *réussite*.

—You are using a card term: *réussite* is a combination of cards that wins at Solitaire. Do you play?

—No, Eric takes care of that.

—In *Sprachgitter*, there is a will toward the impersonal. The grid, the *Gitter*, diffuses the impersonal that is communicated to the reader.

—I would like to buy—us—an ice cream cone, you want one? What flavor do you like?

—Vanilla.

We leave the École Normale, having trudged through the endless lobby. We walk down Rue d'Ulm. He seems to be heading toward Rue Pascal and wants to take the stairs to Boulevard de Port-Royal. We enter the shade of the chestnut foliage, more precisely, of a double row of the sumptuous trees. He likes this sidewalk whose end is out of sight. He likes especially to stop on the platform that looks down on Rue Pascal and gives him the sensation of a hanging garden.

—We have trees above us and the stones of Rue Pascal in their proper place.

We smile because we have witnessed stones flying just a few metres away. Paul says drily:

—You see, when the die is cast, even stones can fly. (He was alluding to a school memory I had told him. The exercise had been to combine 25 verbs with 25 subjects. Speed, appropriateness, dispatch, dash won out over hesitation, and yet, in the end, hesitation came as a paralyzing disaster: 4 words were left, 2 verbs and 2 subjects, and I proclaimed that the cow flies and the swallow ruminates.)

—A while ago, Paul Celan, you talked of a detonation at night that made you think of a cannon shot. Those were your words. You remember?

—Perfectly.

—I heard a detonation like a cannon shot at night.

—Yes.

—What did you think? That your hill was threatened?

—The Contrescarpe was threatened by the detonation. As if hanging over the whole hill were an abstract, unspeakable war, a war without dead, originating in just one shot. By the way, the shot that foretells death is exactly the one that forestalls it, right?

—There is often a muffled detonation in your voice.

—Ah really? You think so?

—I do.

—So there is perhaps a war, or it is the Sagittarius speaking in me.

—Do you mean you choose war?

—No, because even war fits in a cup.

—War as your dice.[17]

—Maybe: a six-sided war for the six-day war. But... what about our vanilla...

We sit down, eat, drink, talk about vanilla ice cream scooped in the form of a ball and of war in the form of dice. He pursues:

—I see a sign here. Both—balls and dice—roll. In fact, the balls of ice cream remain immobile in the cup whereas the dice roll even though they are cubes. But they roll, that is to say they roll away and roll toward. The detonation allows word play with death: it sets a scene... the detonation whose invisible war is reduced to a tone. Strangely, don't forget, the balls of ice cream and the dice share a word: they both come in cups.

—That's ton sur son, tone over sound.

—That's de-ton-ation, so that sound should lead us back to the world, and tone to the sentences we breathe.

A pause, then he goes on:

—Do you know that I read on a wall, in 1968: "The dice won't pass." Who could have written that? What had he loaded his dice with? I've often asked myself.

—No doubt these wall were his dice.

—Perhaps... I'll think about that.

A pause, then he goes on:

—Dice are played forever, thrown forever from their cup... aren't they.

—There is also the idea of a perpetual icon in a die.

—Yes, the die is an icon. You use the word perpetual with the dice. It's true, there is always the question of time, isn't there. Time plunges before us, always... plunges in front of us.

—Why plunges?

—It anticipates for us. Hence the idea of the flash of fire, of lightning connected with dice. The dice plunge, precede us, enact our fate. The faces of the die are the pages of our typographic fate. The book is there, rolling like lightning, its ciphers lighting our way.

The sky is clouding over. We leave.

—We are in the book and we roll... ciphers scattered on the sand.

—And memory is?

—We can't see to the bottom of it.

—You mean the bottom is without matter?

—The bottom has its memory, but we don't have access to it. Access will come one day with a throw of dice. Then the dice will light up another bottom, *ad infinitum.*

—There is no respite at bottom?

—There is no respite at bottom.

Smiles. We have reached the mysterious platform and below, Pascal in his street. Paul asks me:

—Where are you going now?

—I'm going home.

—Would you accompany me as far as my office? I'll give you a copy of my translation of Ungaretti.

At this hour of day, the blue sky casts a baroque red tinge over the bright roofs. Fall is approaching. I find it also in the raspberry cover of the book that its translator hands me. We part.

A child is running over the wet leaves, and the sidewalk of Boulevard Arago is a field of autumn colors. Our steps trace a path in the muddle on the ground. Autumn furtively lets out secret sounds: chestnuts drop, dice are thrown. A mysterious score accompanies the cyphered faces of the landscape, of our conversation.

A little later, we have winter. It's snowing on Boulevard Saint-Michel. Dense snow is falling, and we can't see one meter ahead. The thick white swept by whirlwinds makes walking impossible. We advance in the heart of a hermetically sealed ball.

—In all this snow, the only thing lacking is a white parachute. That alone could help us. Can you imagine, Jean Daive, a parachute opening and floating down through this snow with a man.

—A man.

—A man at the end of his parachute and of our immobile falling.

He laughs. We're slipping. He laughs.

I take on delivering four photos of Paul Celan and copy the last.

We are supposed to meet for coffee in Rue des Grands-Augustins, at André du Bouchet's with whom he has had lunch. I surprise Paul on an impressive Provençal chair—a throne?— peeling a peach, with the juice running all over him who is taken aback by this overabundance. I see his hands encumbered, his lips the color of peach, his eyes laughing, knife and fork crossed, his hazel eyes, the wrinkles on his forehead and embarrassment like a sugar cube on the table.

A first portrait. Beautiful light. He is waiting for me on the sidewalk of Rue d'Ulm. Against the light, I surprise him with his head inclined, listening, his ear glued to an invisible wall: time. He is auscultating time.

Toward the end of the afternoon, in the shade of a chestnut tree, he says:
—Today we cannot talk. But I wonder how we could not talk.

He holds out his hand, and a golden light falls on our approaching fingers. The light disturbs the distance about to decrease to zero, a handshake, golden yellow. He goes on:
—As soon as we talk the world seems to lose some of its solidity, and it's this move toward loss that interests us. But we cannot always face it. It requires an availability that is scorching. What do you think, Jean Daive?

I tell him a conversation I overheard recently. The story is simple: A designer has a certain number of advertising spots to sell. A client buys a space, and the designer closes the deal by stating: the client has been millimetered. I go on:
—According to you, we could possibly millimeter availability. But do you think you could millimeter the sister's garden?
—The sister's garden is out of reach, and a millimeter would not be like a file wrapped in a wet cloth.[18]
—And man?
—He may give in. Sometimes. Precisely when he becomes the client of millimeters. But if you put the human being back into the system of the world, the millimeter's usefulness is naturally reduced to nothing, isn't it.

—And the Surveyor?

—Yes, but he's gone to a field which isn't usually the meter. The Surveyor has to face God, that is, the metaphysical millimeter.

—Checkable.

—To be checked and always uncheckable because Franz Kafka has us read the superposition of yes and no, of the possible and the impossible. Kafka does not write with two hands, but with two pencils in one and the same hand.

—Kafka walks with the Surveyor?

—Kafka walks with the absence of God, hence with the Surveyor. Kafka sleeps and walks. I think I already told you: one night in London, in my hotel room, going to bed, I saw God under the door, a streak of light. I immediately thought of Kafka. There is a God in Kafka and, don't forget, there is a sister.

I feel the breath of the chestnut tree and its sweetness against us. The air is extremely mild, as is the light. I look at our two grayish pink shadows. We walk on.

Late summer afternoon. Washed-out light through the office windows. Washed-out light and the timbreless sound of a drop splashing on porcelain. The drops persist, insist, keep falling. A faucet is leaking, fretting our concentration. Today I superimpose the faucet that does not hold back all the water and the plunge that perhaps dreams of water held in an abyss where the sound of water is joined by what silence can no longer hold back: life. Could a faucet be an absolute observation post or, rather, could a plunge?

I would like to juxtapose the faucet and sugar tongs. Maybe I'll come back to this one day.

—What?

—You are my torment.

I dial the Rue d'Ulm number:

DAN 07.25. Extension 31-30. Immediately I hear a man sobbing, weeping. This man is crying. I have indeed reached Paul's office. I listen: to supplications. I say: Paul Celan. I call. He does not reply. I tell Gisèle.

The Contrescarpe is a village. Grass on the sidewalks. Moss between the cobblestones. Flowers in the windows, and curtains with little red dots. I walk up Rue Lacépède. The top is a few meters away, a few steps. Then I'll see the sea.

—Have you seen Gisèle? asks Paul Celan. Have you called her?

—Yes, I've called and have seen her.

—What is she doing? What did she say? You told her that we had seen each other?

—Yes, I told her we had seen each other and were going to again today.

—Ah. It's good you told her. You'll tell her that we've seen each other, won't you?

—Yes, I'll tell her.

—Call me after you've called her and we'll fix a date. Are you free next Saturday?

Place de la Contrescarpe. Our village. We're sitting on the terrace of La Chope. Edith on my right, a bit frightened of what she has to tell me.

In the distance, in one of the streets of the Contrescarpe I notice Edmond Jabès. He regularly walks for hours in the neighborhood. He walks first in larger and larger circles, then in smaller and smaller, shorter ones. Hands behind his back. His circles have in fact two centers: the Place de la Contrescarpe and the building on Rue de l'Epée de Bois where he lives.

One evening Edith comes back with her shopping bag full of packages and says:
—I've seen him. He does go in circles.

We are side by side in the same café, the Royal Panthéon. Paul asks:
—How did you translate *Heimat*? *Heimat* is an untranslatable word. And does the concept even exist? It's a human fabrication: an illusion.
His eyes and lips sometimes beseeching. More than one entreaty at the bottom of his eyes.

Paul and the neuroleptics.

We are caught in a trap. We look at each other. We are caught in a trap because measuring it does not mean living it.

Chestnuts are dropping. They roll at our feet. Muffled detonations. Far off. It is evening. Autumn. Rolling, bouncing gleam. Spiral depths on the sidewalk. Like mouths opening. We are not talking. Paul Celan remains silent, he almost dances among the implosions he lightly steps over. We move in the poem.

I sometimes confuse snow and cotton.

I dial Paul Celan's number in Rue de Longchamp: POI 39.63. With beating heart.

Under the chestnut trees of Avenue des Gobelins, Paul Celan stops, looks me in the eye and says:

—We are together, you see. We are walking together. And this is strange, isn't it, because our geographies, our ages, our paths are so different. I was born in Czernowitz. You were born in Bonsecours-lès-Valenciennes. The world will remember it because it always remembers poetry. Sooner or later.

One snowy winter afternoon we are walking in the park of Schönbrunn, amorously. Greta and I. Suddenly, at the turn of a path, I find myself nose to nose with a block of cement. It is a pedestal. It carries a sculpture. Greta notices that I am disconcerted:

—Don't be frightened. It's Aeneas carrying his father.

I say to Edith that Paul Celan, Edmond Jabès, and I all walk with our hands behind our back.

—Yes, I had noticed and understood that you were all young graybeards!

I dream that I fell asleep for a few minutes, exhausted, and that I am startled awake. I am on an unknown Greek island. Blue sea. Blue sky and white houses under a terrible sky. A path. A donkey comes toward me. He carries a Christmas tree whose needles seem to be painted green. His eyes are deep and gentle. His smile, knowing. I recognize Greta's eyes. The donkey says to me: "I pine for you." His nonchalant shaking of the tree makes the green paint drop off the needles which turn out to be of yellow metal. A Christmas tree of gold. My hand pets the donkey's gray coat.

Taormina. I take pictures. I get lost in the corridors of the Hotel San Domenico. Suddenly I am face to face with Andreï Tarkovski. In the dark. His hazel eyes are those of Paul Celan.

We look at each other for a long time. Great silence. Absolute, stubborn silence.

The next afternoon. After the projection of Solaris he is sitting at a table in one of the salons of the Hotel San Domenico. It is warm. Dusk. His skinny body. His tortured face, frightening. An absent look, resigned. I stare at him. He turns toward me. Smiles.

We go to Sicily, to Taormina. We cross the Calabrian countryside. We stop en route. For lunch. The place is shady and quiet. Edith puts her two arms on the table, then her head. Edith puts her two arms on the table. They form the letter W. She has fallen asleep. It is noon.

We go to Sicily, to Taormina. I feel it is urgent and do not understand why. We cross the Calabrian countryside. The heat is terrible. Crushing. We stop en route. For lunch. The place is quiet. Shady. Edith puts her two arms on the table. Edith puts her two arms on the table, then her head. Her crossed arms form the letter W. She has fallen asleep. It is noon. I wait. The urgency is still there. I am very worried.

We are at Taormina. We are driving. A poster on an electric pole with the glue still wet announces an hommage to Andreï Tarkovski during the Film Festival.

In the car driving across Taormina, a recollection. One stormy afternoon, a peasant takes his donkey inside a chapel above the Aegean sea and lights two candles. The donkey looks at the chaos outside; he keeps it at bay.

It just dawned on me why it felt so urgent. To go down. Down. Down. Down. Why Sicily? Why Taormina? Why down?

I see Andreï Tarkovski again. I see again *The Mirror.* I see again *Stalker.* I see again *Andreï Roublev.*

I go to his press conference in a salon of the Hotel San Domenico. A crucified body. Frightening silence. He answers the questions like a ghost. "Do you have problems with the Soviet authorities?"—"None."

Taormina. I take pictures. The blue sky. The pink hydrangeas. The sumptuous stairs. I get lost in the corridors of the Hotel San Domenico. I go on. I search. No, I wait. A face. No. Suddenly Andreï Tarkovski. Haggard. His face illuminated. His eyes burning. Again: Paul Celan. Toward me. And his eyes with brownish auburn reflections.

We look at each other. The dark is heavy with the crushing heat outside. We go toward each other. Slowly. He without a sound. Me with apprehension. We pass each other. Great silence. His whole body clenched. He cannot lift his eyes toward the sky. I cannot lift my eyes toward the ceiling. We stare at each other. He smiles at me. "He shall go in and out no other way," writes Saint John.

Every day I go to the Hotel San Domenico. The festival projects its films in a great red hall with drawn curtains. I see again *Andreï Roublev.* I see again *The Mirror.* He is there. Absent. He is there amid an absent audience. Five spectators. Then four. Three. Two spectators. Andreï Tarkovski leads me out. He leads me in.

I surrender to the fire. I surrender to time. I interrupt nothing. I watch *Andreï Roublev.* I watch *Stalker.* He films the earth and what space the soil safeguards when the wet sky pours down on us.

God sings the waters left to the earth's emotion.

I run into Andreï Tarkovski alone in the salon of the Hotel San Domenico. The curtains are drawn. The halflight protects us. A magnetic field holds him in the center of an impenetrable force. He smiles at me. "We have to change our lives," he says to me in English "because people go away without finding harmony, become curt and distressed, and no longer find peace in the always new beauty of the universe."

"People pine for the true life, and I don't want to live any more," he says to me.

"Behind the drawn curtains is the blue sea. It is witness to our efforts toward the spiritual, toward the unknowable."

The Hotel San Domenico is an ancient monastery, and the rooms are the old monks' cells lined up along the long corridors.

Outside the sea is burning. It is our stake. Behind a table in the red salon sits Andreï Tarkovski. He is the level.

To move toward is to move away. The origin remains obscure. I just photographed, in full daylight, a lit electric bulb.

I want to see again the corridors of the San Domenico and look for Andreï Tarkovski.

The reason why I came here is equally the reason why I came into the world: Andreï Tarkovski, Paul Celan and...

We know only the outside of the truth, and possibly its system. Not knowledge.

The corridor is a path. Without lit electric bulb. Without direction. A tunnel dug into the dark. Without flames, without incandescence, without oak, without voice, without sun, without necessity, without precision, without wall.

Walking through the corridors I construct out of need a scene in my mind: Andreï Tarkovski. With angels, visions, curtains going up, dead souls returning, dreams, rooms, libraries, children, burning houses, black suns, gray dogs, naked men.

"In John, there is no mention that time ran backward. In John, there is no mention that the sun was darkened."

In a corridor of the Hotel San Domenico I run across Andreï Tarkovski. His deep eye. Its orbit grows large and I lay my head down in it because its hollow is made by St. John's head in the cave on Patmos where he writes the Apocalypse. Bluff coast. Facing the blue sea. Sea. Grotto. Cave. Orbit. Corridor. Us. John looks at Andreï Tarkovski, an icon. And I pass by. I dream that the gray dogs guard us.

I am there behind the rock. I am behind the volcano. A simple upright giant. I think of the Russian I heard spoken in the salon of the San Domenico. Then of what Paul told me:

—I was no longer writing. I could no longer write. One day in Brest, seeing a Russian flag out in the ocean I saluted the land of Russia with my hand. That was a jolt. The poetry came back, right...

Why would a ceiling be a source of hot water? A bathtub turned over? Mmmm... I am in the bedroom. I photograph the phosphorescent toothbrush.

Edith opens her big black eyes. She smiles. I ask her to pronounce slowly SPI. NO. ZA. She smiles.

Not a breath of air. We are reduced to inert lumps under a crushing sun. The volcano watches. Edith is crying on the beach. The world is a theorem that nobody wants to prove anymore, and I have the feeling the sacred places of the earth are burning before my eyes.

We walk on the beach. We walk in fire. Nothing gives any sign.

I tremble before life. The true laws cannot be known. How to weigh tears?

At night a woman terrorizes me in my dreams. I wake up frightened. She barks.

This woman comes back at night in my other dreams. She strikes me. Bullies me. Beats me. She neutralizes me. I am afraid. I am afraid of myself. I wake up. Gray like a dog. I moan. My gums are bleeding.

The next night she makes me go into a submerged chapel. I am a dog whose peasant-master is called Andreï Tarkovski. I bark under water.

One Thursday afternoon Paul Celan drags me almost by force to a movie house in the Latin Quarter. He wants me to discover *Shadows of Our Forgotten Ancestors* by Sergeï Paradjanov, who on April 25, 1975 will be sentenced to five years in prison for "traffic in ikons and homosexual practices." The film has great power.

The scorching sun on the beach of Taormina. I walk toward the volcano. I see again Paul in the École Normale in Rue d'Ulm. In the middle of the classroom that serves as his office and sometimes his bedroom—he has permanently set up a camp bed near the entrance—he turns in circles, then walks up and down. He has something to tell me. Suddenly he turns to me:

—I have seen *Andreï Roublev.* It's very long…

—It's very beautiful…

—Yes… But Andreï Tarkovski takes the time to tell all. And I think he will one day pay for that, with his life. He should pay for that. Man always has to pay for that.

Edith in tears, as if somebody in her family had died, washing her hair in the bedroom. The light is black. And the water she pours from a pitcher is black.

The hot water of the building comes from the ceiling.

On a terrace, a little girl on her father's shoulders: a polyphony.

"Who multiplies knowledge multiplies pain."

Sumptuous stairs, corridors, thujas, palmtrees, fuchsias, tamarinds, pink hydrangeas. Sun. And the volcano watching. In spite of it all, an end-of-the-world landscape. In spite of it all, we are eating ice cream. I photograph the sea with my first polaroid, and it is black. I photograph a palmtree, and it is out of focus. Ah——

—Why am I hurting and why do I suffer?

—What?

—You are my torment.

"Lord, send me a Master."

We must not mix up times, but I've always simply found myself in the time of those who talked to me.

I look at the Aetna. I recognize the gray dog of my dreams.

When I visited Paul Celan locked up in the psychiatric hospital of Sainte-Geneviève-des-Bois, I noticed a strange Russian church that I find again seventeen years later on the occasion of the death of the film-maker: Andreï Tarkovski is in fact buried in the Russian cemetery of Sainte-Geneviève-des-Bois.

Paris. Edith is at the wheel of her yellow Volkswagen and circles dangerously around the Etoile without really deciding where to go, causing general anxiety, that is to say to CRJ in back and me in front. We talk, we circle. We circle. Once. Twice. A third time. We are nervous about her determined indecision that I am familiar with, and which means that she does not want to drive down the Avenue Victor-Hugo. Suddenly CRJ bursts into a huge laugh:
—In the next life, I'm sure I can say I'll remember this life here.

One afternoon, at the terrace of La Chope, we watch Edmond Jabès approaching, then watch him disappear around a street corner. He comes back into view, moves away. He turns, widening his circles. I am sitting there without moving and stare at a man imprinting his—senseless—rotation on us. I stare at his dance as I stared at the one Paul did in his office.
I tell Edith of my fascination:
—Basically there are those who turn in circles and those who think they don't.
—Sh…
—Only the Jews know that they turn in circles or that they don't because…

—Sh...

—Because they know that in order to turn in circles you have to be upright, but it is also possible to remain sitting...

—Sh...

—The Jews turn in circles for the sake of circling or the Jews don't turn in circles fo the sake of...

—Listen... Be quiet!

—In any case, only the Jews do not turn in circles for the sake of turning in circles because they respond to the call of a universal metabolism. They all turn at the same time by not turning.

—Listen... Leave the Jews alone.

—Or else the Jews turn in order to grind a condition of the infinite. You can imagine what an invisible grinder they hold in their hands.

—I forbid you to continue talking to me about those who turn in circles in order not to!

Ten years after Paul Celan's death we walk along the Seine on a beautiful spring afternoon, Joerg Ortner and I. No. I must tell our day differently. Joerg comes by very early to see me. The morning passes joyfully, and suddenly I insist that we go out and, before we reach the quays of the Seine, pass by the church of Saint-Eustache whose strangeness has always troubled me. It is mild. We walk. Joerg is on my right. He begins:

—You know why you are troubled by Saint-Eustache? Because its strangenes, its construction, its rhythm, is you. Sometimes, Jean, we stand at so complicated and so difficult a crossroad that we stand still for a long time, waiting. And if you do not talk to someone, if you do not address a prayer to someone, you are trapped in a dead-end in the middle of the crossroad. Listen. Are you listening to me? One day, the architect of Saint-Eustache is moping in a café at the market of Les Halles. Imagine him facing a calf's head. He moves a spoon around in his vinaigrette. He eats and is not hungry. He must make a decision. Nothing is working out. How can he go on building when he, the architect, lives in the most terrible confusion? He calls up Palladio in Italy and explains his problem. Palladio replies: "I'm coming" and hangs up. The next morning the two architects discuss matters in the same café at Les Halles. Palladio draws on the paper tablecloth the façade of Saint-Eustache with its extraordinary rhythm of columns, then leaves. It's an ingenious idea because each column seems to be the only one, but always hides another and a third, and you have to understand how the columns add or subtract themselves. It's like your work. If you arrive before the façade and, continuing to walk, look at it sideways, if you mark the farthest column, the column unmultiplies in this rhythm: 1. Then 1, 2. Then 1, 2, 3. Then 1, 2, 3, 4. Continuing to walk around the church you perceive the infinite and start counting it. You understand? And the most ingenious part is that this rhythm of columns is habitable. You said so one day: Saint-Eustache is an example of a habitable façade, of a vertical holy place that is habitable. This means that a repeated column that multiplies the way God unmultiplies can communicate a habitable space. You follow? But why am I saying all this? There was a cross-road. No, I wanted to talk about you. No. Perhaps it's the Seine that pushed me to say all this… No. Ah yes. It's because we never talk about Paul Celan since he died.

Again Taormina. It's evening. The palm trees, the fuchsias and the sea, the long yellow wall of a movie house from the fifties where the Festival is projecting *Stalker*. It is hot. The room is beautiful with its red velvet seats, and the projection begins. The room, where the child with the yellow scarf sits, is trembling. The eyes of the child at the end of the table suddenly flash. Desire? Will? Awareness? Also trembling, a glass that she stares at, bending her head. The child keeps silent. She keeps her silence as she keeps the glass and the world in their trembling. Relief comes from above, cooling our foreheads. Air comes into the theater, and I see a starry sky reaching as far down as the child who affirms her silence by keeping to herself alone the language, that is the trembling of things. God trembles, she seems to tell us, and looking up I see a sliding roof open and push its rectangle into the starry sky. The sky invades the theater and the characters of the film. While I watch the glass trembling on the table I start spontaneously to mumble Letter xii: "Which kind of infinite cannot be divided into parts or can have no parts, and which, on the contrary, has parts, and that without contradiction. Which kind of Infinite can be conceived as greater than another Infinite, without any complication, and which cannot be so conceived."

The world communicates a trembling, but we too tremble. We speak and we tremble. The glass trembles. "The question of the Infinite has always seemed insoluble to all, because they did not distinguish between what must be infinite because of its own nature or in virtue of its definition, and that which has no limits, not indeed in virtue of its essence but in virtue of its cause. And also because they did not distinguish between that which is called infinite because it has no limits, and that whose parts we cannot equate with or explain by any number, although we know its maximum and minimum. And lastly because they did not distinguish between that which we can only understand but not imagine, and that which we can also imagine."[19]

Who are you, Spinoza? You transmit a trembling to our night that goes on, and a shaky glass upsets our peace.

We are walking, and the shade of the trees covers us with a dome, wherein we move and wherein we direct our words. Paul manipulates words while looking, on the imaginary screen of the trees he keeps his eyes on, at his mind's operating field, enlarged or not according to a causal scale that I can sometimes anticipate.

The sky is there, there for the taking, he thinks, across the chestnut foliage.

Huge bouquet of leaves with the sky moving across. A matter of seeing, not taking.

Paradise is there:
—I'm entitled to it, he repeats, I'm entitled.

Today Gisèle is selling the apartment in Rue de Longchamp, on the fifth floor, without elevator. I see again the living room with Paul's desk, his bookcase with its peculiar arrangement, and the dining room that doubles as bedroom.

She moves to my neighborhood, to Rue Montorgueil.

I am critical of André du Bouchet, sometimes severe. Extremely. Paul bows his head. He knows and does not want to hear the arguments. I don't let go. He smiles. We are in Rue d'Ulm or under the chestnut trees of the Avenue des Gobelins or on the Place de la Contrescarpe or in the garden of the Palais-Royal. I insist. He waits out the storm. One day he says to me very quietly:

—André is someone who knows the Littré[20] by heart, he knows the definitions of every word.

And I reply, irritated:
—But that's not the problem…

And yet it is the problem, because the man who lives and entertains all the tensions of a floating language turns from almost biological need toward the man who locks up the word in its most fundamental definitions.

Example: hour—twenty-fourth part of a day.

I especially go back to the remark of somebody I love: words are part of our metabolism.

Contraction of language.
How contract language? Can a definition contract, constrain language?

Paul's stages ("I have to pitch my tent") or stanzas ("I hold my breath"):
The Bukovina—the work camp—Bucarest—Vienna—Paris.

Rue de Longchamp and variants—Rue d'Ulm and variants—Hospitalization and variants—the Seine.

I look at his immense forehead and his ironical smile:
—I am lecturer in German at the École Normal, right…

What does he lay on this "right…," this *n'est-ce pas*… that keeps coming tirelessly, and that he attenuates, weakens, from fear? It holds great fear and terror, as if he were aware that he can, and no longer wants to, convince one last time.

Hands in the pockets of his charcoal jacket, he walks on my left. It's the autumn of rakes and leaves in the Luxembourg gardens:

—There was immediatley... from the publication of "Todesfuge" on, a misunderstanding with Germany. When I went for a reading, right, they all came to meet me at the station, the Germans and the others, the journalists, the Jews and rabbis. Imagine, Jean Daive... the rabbis came to wait for and welcome me... Hosanna, right... Germany's bad conscience had finally found someone to talk to... and no mistake... to talk to... Celebrity is a two-edged weapon because it also puts you under surveillance... and anybody can get it into his head to keep an eye on you and finally say anything... Take the journalists... when they don't know... they just make up things...

"Jean Daive, I blush to want to tell you this: my parents died deported... right... They died over there... and I am here... alive." At the Royal Panthéon.

He orders a third cup of coffee for himself and me.

Words rise to the surface: war, revolt, riot, police action, civil war, State crime, ethnic cleansing, guerilla, disobedience, insubordination, resistance, uprising, dissidence, trouble, agitation, open war, sexual harassment, persecution, slavery, maternal corruption, mmmm...

Muffled steps. Steps in the snow. White is not spoken. Neither at the height of summer nor in the depth of snow.

Muffled steps. Steps among leaves. Autumn is not spoken. Neither at the heart of darkness nor at the heart of fall.

Village of the Contrescarpe, village of Avenue Emile-Zola. He shows me the empty space of the apartment he has just moved into. We make the round. Empty living room. Empty bedroom. Empty kitchen. Empty bathroom. The tub is half full of water and soaking laundry. We go do an errand. Black coats and pants, radishes, salad. Greengrocers' windows with bananas and peaches, faces in make-up, red lips and rosy cheeks. We walk silently. Paul carries an empty netbag.

Dry sentences, no larger than a—folded—handkerchief. Why?

Difficult to think of snow in the heat of a premature summer, which is what I am doing now, what I do often on the Dodecanese Islands: the wind becomes a snow I can think. I walk there. I unfold my handkerchief and walk. A white wall at an angle is drying like a handkerchief in the sun: I walk there. Snow thus equipped with a screen for viewing all of time corresponds no doubt to the shade of trees—the Celanian dome—or the curtain of the double agent. The man who speaks in one language is no longer the one who writes in a different language. Just open *Schneepart* and make a flat count of all the war and espionage terms that Paul read on the "snowy" screen of his mind—(Everything double: *Alles doppelt*): shelter—spike—transit—bullet—vat—debris—rubble—uprising—detector—barricade—tank—microphone—negotiation table—at half-mast—wound—explosive—general strategic situation—warrant of arrest—cables laid, luckily—ammunition—rescue—hatchway—goniometric sights.

The time of *Schneepart* is the perpetual winter of one year: begun on October 18, 1968 it was finished on December 22, 1969. A year, a winter of *alles doppelt*: the actual riot puts in perspective the riot of language across stammers. The actual rubble is also the rubble of verse. This man chews his writing.

This man confronts war because he has swallowed the verb. This man, that is, the hangdog, the epileptic, moves through a density of words from which the verb is absent.

One summer I reread *Lichtzwang*. He wrote this book with a Driver's Manual in his hand.

In late afternoon we go into a café. Our table faces a mirror. Paul Celan:

—Do the mirrors bend over us, over our distress? Man is no longer man. Man no longer speaks. Man no longer is. Man no longer is upright. He is no longer anywhere. The poet can only qualify him.

—That's why you tell me that mirrors bend over man. The mirrors bend over adjectives that account for absence…

—of a trace… of a memory. Yes, man is gone along with the verb. All that's left are nouns, substantives. The subject remains, but the subject is almost no longer conjugated.

—You mean to say that you turn the noun into a verb?

—Yes. The noun reflects man.

—The subject includes the verb, the subject is the mirror of man.

Paul looks at the café mirror. He lowers his eyes. Again, stubborn silence.

Later. Avenue Emile-Zola. Empty apartment. Light and emptiness. The long table. We go out. The farmer's market. Sidewalks, streets, legs and black stockings. We clear a path. Paul walks holding his netbag with five grapefruit scrupulously selected by their stamp of origin: Jaffa.

The stamp at the bottom of the net turns on his hand.

Note: five grapefruit in his net and five floors to climb in Rue de Longchamp.

Commotion in the trees. Commotion behind the fence of a garden going to seed. Paul resumes:
—How to open up to the light the Old and New Testaments? How to unify them into One? The poem should say, should show this superposition.
—Messiah or Savior, they ride on vision, that is, on the poem.
—You notice I used the word *ajourer*, to open up, break open, to the light.
—Yes, I heard... the sacred texts are pierced by the light in various ways.
—The sacred texts and the figures in the sacred texts are pierced by the light in various ways... I mean that luminous, miraculous punctures, the stigmata of sacred texts, reach even the poem. We write with luminous wounds that illuminate our hands.
—But what do you see through these openings?
—The effects of double language. The effect of my resistance to the language I am now speaking with you, which is not that of the poem. My resistance makes gaps of light in the sacred text.
—Mmmm... I wonder if we need a double language in order to read the Old Testament and the New?
—Mmmm... a double language in order to understand, to take in two lives: the Old and the New. The poem is a wheel that makes the two others turn round.

Long silence. We silently observe each other. Paul closes in on himself, silently touches the depth of his meditation. His fingers tremble, his lips tremble. Paul goes on:
—Have you ever observed a ruined wall and how a ruined wall can turn into a living heap of stones and pebbles, as if

the ruined wall could become for us the form, the life that we lack?

—Mmmm…

—And yet this life is lifeless. The wall is in ruins and the heap is in ruins, two parallel and empty lives. It's as if I compared a ruined wall with a niche… Have you ever observed a niche?

—Mmmm…

—Well, the niche remains empty. There is a dog in the bedroom, and the child manipulates this stage house in his dream: he sits in front of the niche and, in his head, barks. I've often noticed that a taciturn object—the house for the child—leads us to a luminous object—the niche. Two roofs maintain an emptiness that chases the sky out of the house or encases it in the niche.

—Mmmm…

—A hospital helps you to look at, to think the world beyond the wall, beyond the hedge. All you need is to jump, and you cannot do it: the medication plasters you to the floor. There used to be walls and hedges. You noticed that at Sainte-Geneviève-des-Bois there are not even any hedges: just a large circular meadow and around it a wire at knee-height. You cannot walk long on the meadow, let alone step over the wire. But you can still think.

—Of privet hedges that grow oranges.

—That's where we must carry the world, whether we sit on a chair or have our head on a pillow. Suddenly you carry the world without arms, with just a bit of smoke. Then suddenly the world bounces before you on the grass, over the wire.

—Mmmm… You think the world carried this way can be a guide?

—The poem is not necessarily a provisional guide like the world.

—Mmmm...

—Don't forget. Somewhere there is the wolf, and the wolf devours everything: the provisional, the guide, the crutch, I mean the provisional or even the crutch of the provisional and the crutch of the guide. You know, the wolf does not stutter.

—Mmmm... If I understand right, you are looking for an occasion for yourself and the wolf.

—We are the wolf because we no longer stutter while eating nor perhaps while speaking.

—I expected you to say while writing.

—We still stutter while writing...

—...because the wolf does not write.

—We have come to superimpose the wolf and the guide and to hear the guide in the wolf's belly stuttering the provisional. He strikes with his crutch. He strikes and counts the blows and stutters, and the crutch is the occasion of the stutter, and I answer you: I am the occasion of the wolf and I am the occasion of the stutter.

—You are not the occasion of the guide because the crutch...

He interrupts:

—Because the crutch is a writing tool in snow, in grass, in sand. There is, isn't there, writing that is stutter and limp. Let me tell you that there is writing that is crutches.

His smile is luminous, radiant. He goes on:

—Stuttering presents our asymmetry of the world and to the world. It is the birthmark on the rosy cheek of the sleeper. Stuttering is the occasion of speech, an occasion gambled, really gambled with dice by the moment of speech. There is... how to put this?... an interruption... or a... switching... commuting a switch... Crutches interrupt the current... the current life... absent the current life. The stutter cuts and can reestablish the current and is in itself an outlet of current, but also a draft of air in our current life. Have you ever noticed

133

the ramp that runs parallel to an escalator, I mean the hand-rail… limping disturbs the occasion of the handrail: it stops, marks a stop at the moment the wounded foot limps, the wound imposes its timing on the step… the handrail marks and misses our time… because the handrail… it's you or me… and my hand gripping the handrail is the memory of the intermittent wound of the world set down on the ramp… the hand of stutter and limp.

—So poetry is not the handrail.

—Poetry does not run or rail, and poetry does not rail with or on hands.

With these words, Paul Celan closes in. He falls silent. We fix a date. We separate.

Summer on the Cyclades. The pears above the tables of the café are not yet yellow. They are heavy. They are. I look out beyond the fields at what could be the Aegean. The island is calm. I am not reading. I am not counting. I breathe with open mouth. I remember.

He tells me he is shortly leaving for Israel. I read worry in his face. But his face is very gentle. We meet again and say goodbye.

A postcard sent from Jerusalem: Affectionately. Paul Celan.

A panorama of the City with its blue sky, its golden domes and its sacred stones.

On his return we meet again in Rue d'Ulm:

—I gave a talk that I wrote over there… You would call it a vegetative talk… It's very long… Look… I wrote all these lines and am the first to be astonished... Here, I give you this copy of the talk.

The day after Paul's supposed disappearance, a friend stands under the apartment windows in Avenue Emile-Zola. He calls: "Paul, Paul." Then, when there is no sign, he goes to the bedroom windows and starts singing the Israeli anthem.

After long years of struggling with the poem, and this includes the years of childhood and adolescence, I send the manuscript of *Décimale blanche,* finally finished or almost, to Paul Celan. A whole year goes by without a reaction. Then I get a note from André du Bouchet that he read my text in "Rue de Longchamp" and wants to publish it in the first number of the magazine *L'Ephémère.*

I do not reply. Some weeks later, a letter from Paul Celan: "I think I have been indiscreet. I beg your pardon. Give me a call." I telephone. "Ah, it's you," and we meet.

The story continues: *Décimale blanche* appears in Number 2 of *L'Ephémère.* André du Bouchet proposes to publish the entire text with Mercure de France: "Your first book," he says, and I say: "No."

A few days later, near the paulownias of the Contrescarpe, Paul Celan admits that he understands my concern and my refusal:
—I hear you've said no... Jean Daive, sometimes we must transform a no into a yes. I ask you. Think it over... Let's eat some hot chestnuts. There is a stand not far from here.

We walk peeling the chestnuts... Smiles. Looks. The chestnuts burn our fingers. We blow on them.

In the end, *Décimale blanche* is published by Mercure de France.

Paul Celan continues a conversation:
—We talked the other day, you talked the other day about the spirit of place. It's true, there is such a thing as the genius loci, isn't there... For example, us: we have been divided, cut off, separated by an invisible, political barrier. That is, the most remote border goes back to the most remote border... As if the least visible border became in spite of all the most noticeable and marked with a redhot iron: one and the same language on both sides of the barrier. I was born in Czernowitz, you were born in Bonsecours-les-Valenciennes, as I like to say... And here we are. Note that I don't say... here we are in a fine mess.

Where I come from? Who I am? Where I'm going? I won't try to answer or, rather, I'll try to answer along a parallel by telling bits of a story. I'll talk about Paula—my mother—the feminine of Paul. Paula is the daughter of Jules, who is the son of Jules, and Paula's father has a son Jules, my uncle and Paula's brother. The first or oldest Jules was a paver, that is he paved roads and, knowing the family, I can assure you that he paved the hell of the North with delight, cruelty, and perfection. This particular hell still exists, around Thivencelle, Blanc-Misseron, Escaudin, since we are driving there and it is nowadays "classified." What does hell consist of? What is a paving stone, a series of paving stones on the surface of hell, become unnegotiable for humans? A first answer, because Paula refers back to Paul: the paver is the one who sets up, thinks up, hobbling. Another answer: the paving stone refers to the word, i.e. to stammering. Driving over paving stones you can't talk except in stammers. I'll continue my family history. The oldest Julien was a paver. The last but one—Paula's father—was a contractor in roads and bridges: he had transformed the paving stone into an excessively prosperous business. I stress the word "excessively," because it led to the end of the Jules: the last hanged himself with a clothesline in the attic of a hunting lodge. End of the road. I have often thought about the role of the road, I much observed, as a child, the uninterruptedness of the roads. I looked at the layers of materials and when I then looked at the surface I could not help seeing in my mind the hidden construction. I must write the word incest. Why? Because roadwork transforms a negotiable surface into hell, and this totally paved hell becomes our natural road, and our always intellingent thinking hands us the necessary patience or will or crutch. Incest is in the paving stone. It is in the family (I observed it) and in the paving stone. Incest is. How? I am the one who has changed the paving stones into dice. The dice are in the poem. The die is incest. I gamble for you. I don't roll for you. Incest does. It precedes us: paving stone or die, Paul or Paula. Road and hell. Roads don't arrive because incest or poem lend a helping hand. But I am superimposing Paul and Paula as I live superposed, as I see superposed sentences and roads according to a mix of blood and geography: the articulations of incest are identical, implacably. I again see the foreman, Désiré, build a road across open fields in the snow: paving stones, sand, sacks of cement, and unknown women in the snow, in the open fields, bringing the men wine, tobacco, bread, warm tarts. And later, the same road farther on, toward the height of summer under a scorching sun, and the same women dressed very lightly, with heavy breasts. The field is torn up and the loves of a road across fields are torn and reborn farther off. Unknown women, neighbor women, neighbors of a road under construction, they all walk along the road. For them the way still goes through the fields, like making love in the fields. Looking at the paving and at the group of people I think, even as a child, that the poem varnishes a universal, amorous geography: a complicated pottery

—The courtyard leading to our garden. Which caused a huge scandal. I taught the family that what was paved, cemented, sealed and paved, could also be unpaved. It was on a Sunday during the interminable lunch. The quiet of the garden, of the children alerted the family who suddenly saw the havoc.

—The art of paving goes through the ages... Through texts and ages. The art of paving is also an art of the hand. What are in these days of non-communication the objects of the hand? Easy to enumerate: the pen, the pear, the paving stone... You see... I find words starting with P. But tell me your Sunday.

—Atrocious.

—Your family Sunday.

—Imagine a long table with the family, a perron, the garden, and two children grappling with subtracting stones: an impeccably paved surface and two children's voices whispering: minus 13, minus 14, minus 15... the 57th alerted them.

—And then?

—You can imagine how offended they were. Their ethic was offended.

—But what was your problem? Why did you unpave?

—I wanted to unpave an idea because it was unbearable to me that the first yards of the garden were paved, precisely those that led to the strawberries and to the rows of peartrees with the gooseberries in between. So, one Sunday, I wanted to modify the access, make it...

—Yes, I see... one day presence comes to imply its absence. One day the stone's in your hand. One day the stone's in nothing.

—Mmmm... You are saying something else...

—I am weighing all the possibilities of the paving stone.

—The only thing and the most real is family.

—Yes, the paving stone is no longer in the pool: it is in the families, star-spangled. Stones come to families because like the skies they have lost all their stars. And man comes to make up for it... Starry pavement...

Paul Celan murmurs "starry pavement" and asks:

—How can a paving stone multiply into hell, by this I mean into the handrail?

—The invisible...

—The invisible handrail.

—Being universal, a paving stone can multiply even into hell.

—Ah... yes.

—Because it is indivisible and incurable.

—Ah... yes... invisible... indivisible... in-curable...

I'll think about that... I'll leave you now... Give me a call!

Seasons go by. A few. One day, Paul Celan tells me he has written to Heidegger.

—I've read much Heidegger. I've much annotated his books. I just wrote him. I don't expect a reply.

A few weeks later:

—I'm going to Germany. To meet Heidegger. I hope he'll hear me.

Later:

—In Todtnauberg there is a fountain crowned with a starry die, and I thought about our conversation. Do you remember our starry pavement?

—Yes.

—Well, I saw it again at Heidegger's, I met him in his forest full of paths that go nowhere.

—Paths that go nowhere...

—*Holzwege...* according to Heidegger... right...

—And children go everywhere...

—Without a path... like poets... they go everywhere... and like some other philosophers... like us... right... we go to the barracks of the camps, the cafeterias of hospitals... and we look at the wire that we don't step over...

He smiles. He goes on:
—I had illusions. I hoped to be able to convince Heidegger. I wanted him to talk to me. I wanted to forgive. I waited for this: that he find words to trigger my clemency. But he maintained his position. Germany is strange... another pavement... indivisible.
—And yet divided.
—The division is invisible... I deeply believe this... And this comes out in Heidegger's work and maybe in his thought... an invisible division whose vocabulary escapes... Germany altogether. Of what is this division made? How to heal it? Prayer? Waiting?

Perplexed silence. He goes on:
—I've written a poem over there that I'll show you. The occasion of the meeting was a poem that is vegetative, that is, neither open nor closed, having only language for opening and closure. It contains prayer, waiting.
—You say the division is invisible because it is everywhere.
—Yes, the division has made fissures in every meter, every individual down into his words.

After a long silence, he continues:
—The forests are very old. The forests are older than man. They have seen the gods die. And man is naked in a forest of dust, dry leaves and roads covered with leaves and dust.

A long silence, then he continues:

—Verse breathes all that and on all that. Man wants to conquer and conquest wants gold. I've always thought the poem should cross out the world. You know engravers are supposed to cross the plates once the edition is printed. Yes, the poem should cross out the world. The poem is a diagonal that crosses out the world just as syntax is the diagonal of the poem. Next time, I'll bring you "Todtnauberg."

Mild air. Gray-blue sky. The gray stone of the facades lights up the depth of the streets. We walk along the Seine. Paul Celan looks at Notre-Dame. An empty barge glides on the green water. He mumbles:
—An orphan.

All during this walk, he seems determined to maintain silence between us. I see again very clearly Paul Celan's gray shape under the snow. He crosses the Place du Palais-Royal in the wind and whiteness. His body is suffering, heavy, powerful, and I add to this vision his will not to speak: the incomplete within the complete.

He keeps silent because there is a mumured conversation going on which he must be hearing. He maintains silence because there is speech unfolding that he must arrange as opening or closure. His silence is an electric switch.

We walk along the fence of the Luxembourg garden. The late afternoon is mild. It's autumn. Paul Celan talks without fear, even jokingly.
—Don't forget that a poem is always a letter to the father.
—Mmmm...
—I often think of Franz Kafka's "Letter to the Father."
—...which he did not send...

—At the request of his sister Ottla...

—...no: of his mother...

—A woman is a woman... right...

—You mean...

—I mean she implores.

—And Franz Kafka hears her implore him?

—He doesn't send the letter to the father or have it delivered to him, right...

—Who is the father in the "Letter to the Father"?

—God is present and the judgment of men and no doubt all the misery of the son...

—The son who paces the threshold of his father's house, who measures how far the door opens... and anyway, what is a door that does not really open?

—Or a door that only seems to open and never really does! I know... I know that very well...

We are still walking along the fence of the Luxembourg. He starts over after a long silence:

—You were looking at the rakes, right...

—I am looking at the garden and the rakes.

—Rakes make me think of Charles Baudelaire...

—Yes: of Baudelaire and the autumn of ideas. It's raining. The garden soil is hollowed out.

—The water hollows and the rakes arrive.

Prague in spring. We are looking for Franz Kafka in the streets he used to walk. I search in the faces of the crowd for his sister Ottla, for her eyes, and Greta has an expression of deep sweetness. Greta is calm, loving, lascivious in her brown wool suit with black checks.

She makes us visit the rooms of the National Museum. In a strange, almost worrisome state, she explains a painting by

Gustav Klimt: a garden with large red flowers, she tells me, and a meadow of which the Viennese painter keeps only a memory. A tree and a woman with exuberant hair made of gold squares. She continues:

—A woman is waiting in the first garden, the one that is life because it comes before everything. The hair is solar, the grass is green, the flowers are red. This woman's dream is everywhere, this woman's waiting is everywhere. And yet nature does not wait. So a woman in the deepest solitude can say: I am very near you.

We walk toward our hotel. In the room, which is huge, I think of the hair of this woman who is waiting. Greta is at the dressing table looking at the mirror, once again upset by the strangeness of her face:

—How ugly I am, she sighs.

I think about Franz Kafka's insomnia. He is alone at night, at a table. He writes. And L.'s face comes to me, who spends her nights of insomnia reading Franz Kafka.

Then I think how Greta one day said to me in despair:

—I know I should not, but I'm going to do it.

In the end, she did not.

At L.'s place, rue Saint-Maur, one Friday night:

—You'll tuck me in? You'll say goodnight? she asks.

—I'll tuck you in. I'll say goodnight...

—My body wants you. My vulva wants you.

—I'll tuck you in and go.

—Yes, tuck me in... I want to love you. I don't want to orgasm. Stay a little longer.

—I'm leaving. Go to sleep. Talk to your insomnia, put it to sleep.

—If I can't sleep I'll read Kafka. I'd like to go to Prague with you. Do you know Prague?

—Mmmm...

Rue Saint-Maur. L. in my arms says:

—I can kill you.

—...

—I can kill you.

—...

—I'd like to kill you.

—...

—There would be no witnesses.

—...

—Nobody would know.

—...

—I am using a false identity. I could kill you.

—...

—I am sad. You make me sad. You don't say anything. Talk to me... Answer or I'll hit you!

—...

—I'm sad.

— ...

—It's true, I'm sad. I'm unhappy. I don't sleep. Because of you I don't sleep anymore... I can't fall asleep. I have to read Kafka all night and "The Hunger Artist" does not make me laugh at all...

—...

—And you don't even know how to talk to women.

Autumn again. I push a door. I push a second door, I push a third door. At the end of this labyrinth I am in Alain Veinstein's office. He is sitting at his desk, feverish, haggard. I ask if he needs anything. His hands seem to hold an invisible object. A shovel? A rake?

—Sometimes I dream I'm dead and looking for my grave, he says.

Prague at night. Stone staircases. Ramps. In the Street of the Alchemists Greta looks as if she were hallucinating. Her eyes pierce what she sees. I'm getting afraid.

We must separate the yes from the no (Paul Celan). We must separate the mattress from the box springs (Edith).

Prague in spring. In the hotel room. The curtains are drawn. It's night. We are lying across the bed. In our clothes. I have my coat on. Greta, her jacket and boots. She falls asleep or pretends to. Paul Celan's letter is on the dressing table. It isn't quite night yet.

I stare at the ceiling with its fake Venetian chandelier. A memory surfaces. I went to surprise Greta at home, in Vienna. At that time she was living with her mother in a development flat. The two women shared the same bedroom and slept in twin beds of lemonwood:

—Before going to sleep we read out loud Trakl, Celan, Kafka... One night, my mother said about Celan: "But this is the voice of a sister I hear there..."

—You are anxious, Paul Celan?
—No, upset rather than anxious. I go to Berlin tomorrow...
—To Berlin?

—I take a plane to Berlin tomorrow. I'll see the Wall, the Spree river, the hotel Eden. I'll be thinking of you.

A few days later, Gisèle tells me:
—Paul caused a veritable scandal in Berlin. He abruptly left the table during an official dinner. Left the cultural attachés, guests, publishers stranded. Just got up and left.

People say of the sun that it's bright, dimmed, new. Today it's raining. It is an autumn of floods.

We are walking toward the Luxembourg. We are in Rue de Condé. Walking toward the fountain of Marie de Médicis:
—A great lover, Greta whispers in my ear.

I hold up the umbrella and take her arm. I tell her my definition of a sister:
—A sister would still look for what has not really disappeared.
—A sister would wear mourning, she replies.

The basin of the Médicis fountain always seems strange, neglected with its mass of soaked leaves, and out of the way.
—This basin is like my face… You have to look at it for it to feel, live, love in spite of the acne which is my ordeal.

Rain. We walk. The trees and their foliage above us.

A golden sky stretches over the fall.
—Kafka does not measure in order to overcome logic, says Paul Celan. He measures in order to speak to the human being, unaware that the human being is finally nothing but suffering. And the absurd idea to want to measure it, to want—no pun intended—to account for it… count it.

I still remember a remark of L.'s:

—I had gotten to a point in my life where all that was left to do with my days was to buy, buy anything with stolen checks.

My mother is elegant. Why? It's a spring day. We walk through a dark alley that looks out at fields and vast meadows. My mother is pregnant with my sister. We enter a dank house with a dirt floor. An old toothless woman greets us. The two women turn aside, disappear. Why? I am waiting in a room. Under the door, daylight forms a phosphorescent streak. I feel uneasy. I am seven. I tell Paul Celan about my distress.

—At that time I was in Vienna, he replies, I was on my way toward Paris, toward the Contrescarpe.

—Yes… and my sister was not born.

My mother's hand in mine against a background of yellowish light. A dark alley with ruts, unpaved. Distant fields covered with coal dust because we are right in the mining basin. And ladies' shoes in a landscape of nettles. All this does not distress me. There is also a child there with a scooter, always the same, little Michel, a miner's son. He tries to fly a kite. His attempts let a big red lozenge appear in the opaque sky.

—Hosanna, interrupts Paul Celan. And where is this happening? You told me you were born in the North, near the border, at Bonsecours.

—Yes… and the distress I am talking about is tied to a village where, on Thursdays of my first years of childhood, I visit Mireille, my first love, who plays the cello and is the daughter of an incestuous union of a brother and sister, Jean and Jeanne. This takes place at Pâturages… in the mining basin.

—At Pâturages?…

—Yes… Will you permit me to tell you an anecdote which gets us away from the unease… and recenters it?

—I'm listening, Jean Daive.

—When I arrive in Paris, in bad shape and reduced to total silence, I decide two things: to read all books and see all films. So I go to the Bibliothèque Nationale from 9 in the morning till 6 in the afternoon and then to the Cinemathèque in Rue d'Ulm from 6:30 till midnight. One day in Rue des Écoles, I notice a poster saying: a classic of world cinema: *Verts Pâturages, Green Pastures.* My heart seemed to stop. I run there. And what do I see: people... black people wearing white angel wings and singing in paradise, in American... Their feet on a cloud... They are in heaven and... they dance...

—Ha! Ha! Ha! Jean Daive, stop, please, you make me laugh too hard... Green Pastures indeed... Ha! Ha!... Speaking of your coal-black Pâturages.

I watch a tree floating in the sea off Santorini. Homer says, a tree dragged from the mountain top by a donkey is born to sail on the waters. Twice I got lost in the same forest. The beech trees appear and grow larger like smoke. They suffocate the lost child who, advancing and not advancing, becomes an unflinching dike and tears through the shadows.

—Your Médicis fountain, Paul Celan replies, whose mass I admire, juts out like a dike. I agree. Nevertheless it is like us— in perfusion.

The Médicis fountain by a black fence at the edge of an adjoining street: the rosyfingered Great Lover keeps watch, and I look at the Aegean in the fountain basin full of drenched leaves.

Paul Celan loves its size, its proportions, the mass of its plant vault, its goldfish.

L. once said to me: "I came like a guy. Now I'll turn my back, smoke, snore. And it's a great lover talking to you."

Sleep asks me if I'm asleep, if I want anything. I reply that I'm no longer asleep and want nothing.—Listen! it commands. Do you want to arm your city and defend its walls?—But I have no city to defend.—I'm aware of that, but I know you count on the infinite.—That has nothing to do with defending walls that have not seen me being born.—It's never too late: birth lies ahead. I want you to get up. I want you to run along these anthracite shores and fly your kite above the green pastures. Then your city will be crushed by a permanent atypical pain.—Who are you?—I'll come back and tell you.

The Seine runs all the way to Charenton in front of the cement works, but it has two arms. I watch it flow away. I am on the fifth floor of a clinic where I wait to be cured. On the table three roses about to open, and the Seine flows through their radiance.

—Why were you at Pâturages? asks Paul Celan.

—The punishment that was Bonsecours was not enough for my parents. For themselves. They looked for even more punishment at Pâturages, tried to create a kind of inexhaustible reservoir of mortifiaction. Why? To forget life.

—Ah. I think I understand… So that you would not forget it, you, Jean Daive.

—Can I tell you a story?

—Yes, I'm listening…

—One day a tired Michelangelo Antonioni stops his car on some godforsaken village square. He sees an empty café. He goes in. Sits down. A young woman, beautiful, unhappy, miserable, behind the bar. He smiles at her. They exchange first looks and first words. Antonioni asks her first name. She says: "Delitta—delitta from delict, crime, with an a because I'm a girl." Embarrassment. And a long silence. Antonioni is troubled. She comes to his aid. "My father loved my mother, but

150

did not want a child. She begged him. Well then, our child will be called Delitta."

—What a mark of horror and what bitterness against life… Yes… this story is terrible, murmurs Paul Celan.

Sleep bends over me and warns that it'll disturb my sleeping.—You sleep because you don't have the guts to fight your own dividedness, says sleep.—I am divided?—You think you are indivisible and you are as divided as possible. Night has come, and according to you we must obey it. The reason is simple. Waking does not keep you in your self-inflicted punishments that you taste drop by drop like a refreshment.—I've heard that before, right?—Don't abandon your city! Save it. Defend its walls. Protect it.—Why fight when it's enough to set it on fire and burn it all? A city is not a woman.—Troy was. Think about it. Troy was the most beautiful—And most destroyed.—Most burned in fact.—So? Woman or fire?—I'm leaving, I don't want to wake you.—I think I've seen your jaw before.—I'll be back.

Childhood again told near the Médicis fountain, childhood and its meadows black with coal dust, its steep, almost vertical alleys, and a whole village of crooked houses resting on pits and working levels that subside and sometimes collapse. We are still on the surface, sigh our neighbors Luther and Hortense. I am eating my soup in a large, bright room when the marbled cement floor opens before my eyes. I say: "Hello, fissure!" And go toc! toc! toc! on the table with my spoon. The house is moving. The furniture shaking. The world growling. Two places at the table remain empty. My father is not there. My mother is not there. My sister was not born. A weight acts on the house and all the fissures divide it into infinitely small portions. I look at the gleaming vegetables in my soup while the destruction from the ground is preparing scientifically. One day everything will give way, and the house split apart, but the sky will remain above us, veiled by what lets a child with a scooter take wing: a kite flying high in the air.

The house is fecund in shocks not of the heart: but the void. There is no certain truth except in the wake of untruth. I rely on the truest judgment of the real because my life is lived in the wake of the negative. The heart is hidden. And I don't live there.

What remains hidden in the house? A menace can—strike —at any moment. But I have a refuge. One room has no purpose and is not really used. I have pushed a desk under the only window, which looks out on the street. The desk is an airplane that I pilot and make fly. I pass my days lying in it, in front of dials, dashbord, and already sophisticated mechanisms. I fly missions. I bomb cities. My plane is hit. I parachute. My plane burns. I am made prisoner. I go down the sky, down life upside down.

—Basically, sighs Paul Celan, what difference is there between your imaginary games in a paternal desk and the spade with which I dig in a work camp. The password, most often unconfessed, is: extermination, and the idea is always the same: the ones who give life order death. And our suvival, Jean Daive, we owe, just barely… to exposing our resistance. For us, it's language and a different poetry. Come, let's go back to the Contrescarpe and the paulownias that you love. Did you have a garden back home?

—Yes, there was a weeping ash, a privet hedge…

—Ah…

—Through which I crept to visit Luther and Hortense… my adoptive family.

The time spent inside the paternal desk is the time of stability. I no longer have to be terrified, waiting for the fissure to move toward me.

I've locked the doors, I lie on my back, I look at the dashbord, I calculate and program the trajectory of a catastrophy. The targets have to be reached across states of unbalance. A screened lamp is the moon: it lights the discontinuous transition in process, progress, that finally hits. What? No doubt an Empire whose distant *Bang* I hear!

—All this is absolutely biblical, says Paul Celan. And I wonder if we do not develop in a density, to use your own term… that is a projection of the Bible. Our most daily gestures, our simplest, most normal gestures are charged with our memory of the Bible without us really being aware of it. We come out of the Bible, we are the Bible. And is my spade not the manometer of all times?

In summer silence we walk up Rue des Carmes. We walk along a palissade: it fences in a wild garden and a house with walled up façade. Cries come from inside the walls. We meet a clochard. His feverishness makes us think he is joining the others. Paul Celan says:

—A clochard is a person who closes houses.

—But the houses are not born.

—Verse is our house.

—You think verse has been born.

—The house has been born, verse has been born.

—Verse has been born, or verse exists?

—Verse has been born: it is a birth, isn't it… a perpetual birth… you'd say.

The Place de la Contrescarpe appears, a luminous dark green. The three paulownias fill the space. He asks me to accompany him. "Accompany me," and we take Rue du Pot-de-Fer onto Rue Tournefort.

I'll leave him in front of his building where, with perfectly controlled embarrassment, he'll suggest I don't come up because the cleaning woman didn't come today. Then I'll walk back toward center city putting together woman and cleaning. Does writing clean? Does writing belong to woman? A voice asks me to stop.

I would like to analyze the politeness of Paul Celan. I would like to analyze politeness in Paul Celan. Analyze the difference between of and in. First of all it is a permanent state (of), but above all an alert, a *qui-vive* (in). It allows Paul to control his silence with sufficient sensitivity. His silence is a third ear. And politeness is its almost metaphysical material. Red meat is accompanied with port. Salt with sugar, on the coast of an internal sea. Politeness is morbid self-protection, as if the word alone were not enough to authorize communication. Does the heart not feel the world too keenly without the presence of politeness... right? Does it not accompany the way a glass of port does red meat? Politeness plays a large part in approaching the world: economy joins acumen. Paul turns to me:
—Have you noticed this woman with the brown purse? She is watching us. She watches us watching her, and she's drinking the same thing we are. The square is between us. But I wonder if we can watch her unpunished?
—What is missing in your watching?
—She certainly didn't invite me to.
—An invitation's missing?
—An invitation for two to watch.
—Why did you mention the fact that she's drinking what we are drinking?

—I was hoping to reassure myself, express the space of an invitation, i.e. an implicit reciprocity. Before finding the error I wanted to formulate scruples. In the first moment between two persons, the unknown is surrendered by both at the same time. Seduction comes later, after politeness. Politeness is the road to seduction.

—And what she drinks is the road...

—What we drink, what she drinks is the road to reciprocal attention.

Paul Celan always, in a flash, notices the mechanism in human behavior, the conception, the rituals, to which he reacts with sociable urbanity. It is in a very confidential moment that Paul Celan suddenly changes the subject and violently reproaches me:

—At André du Bouchet's you were ill at ease...

—Ah.

—During the conversation you kept running your finger over a knife blade.

—Yes, I remember.

—I often wondered for what reason.

I remain dumb because I understand that politeness is also made of critical moments like this one, as borderline as a guard's *qui-vive*—where crossing, even internalized, becomes apocalyptic. Another example. I enter his office at the École Normale Superieur one winter evening. It is 8 PM. He is waiting for me. I know, I sense that waiting has been a trial. I see that he has fought with himself. I approach, he does not hold out his hand. He is in a panic. I know this panic. I approach one centimeter at a time. The few meters between us are a barrier of fire. I see that he may explode in spite of his impeccable, perfectly neutral attitude in his dark suit. I suddenly realize that he is staring at my black tie and in his mind tries to change it. My firmness gets through to him as friendly and suddenly relaxes the encounter. He holds out his hand, smiles, and points at my black tie.

—Are you wearing a black tie for me?

—No, but I could not change it.

—Ah.

—I wear it for a friend who died and whose...

—Yes... I invite you to dinner.

All during the meal, Paul Celan gives in to a dazzling seductiveness mixed with, and held in check by, anxiety.

A word comes back to me today that he taught me "to manipulate with caution."

—All words have a life. Some more than others. It's our happy or unhappy relation to words that determines the harmony of vision and syntax.

—Johannes Poethen's vocabulary reminds me of Gottfried Benn's "Morgue."

—It's a vocabulary of decay. Medicine is part of life. Decay is part of life. Death is part of our limbs. Limbs and the decay of limbs are part of resurrection.

—Mmmm...

—A strange Sunday I'm having you spend here, right... Translation and the seventh day.

—Mmmm...

—All in front of Poethen's poems.

Johannes Poethen's obsessive word, to be manipulated with caution, is: inoculate.

The following Sunday we continue to discover Johannes Poethen's vocabulary. Paul Celan signals refusal, distance, perhaps rejection. He remains deliberately absent. I sit at the table; he, at a slant, both hands on the table top. His lips move. Then his right hand and thumb hold his left wrist. Time passes. He counts the time. His lips move. I gather that Paul Celan is taking his pulse and counting. Episode of a translation.

—For it is said, thou shalt translate on the seventh day.
—In which passage of the Bible is this written?
—A passage in my head.
—Ah.
—The seventh day is the day of language in pure suspense.
—And what does language do during the six preceding days?
—It gives in to duplication.
—You mean speaking doubles the world?
—Speaking doubles the world... yes.

Remains the sparkling of words in a chilly room, and a beating pulse. I see the thumb almost dig in. I see the thumb searching. And I see myself alone before the words, a searcher for meaning on this seventh day. Paul Celan almost deliberately searches for his pulse while looking at me. And I plunge my eyes into the medical book. "Inoculate." "Yes, to be manipulated with caution." Suddenly my heart starts to race, and the room, and the book. The cold calms me down. Paul looks at me. I translate. Inoculate. Etc. Resurrection is not for tomorrow without... my eyes search the room for Franz Kafka's sister, and, bizarre, she starts to talk to me. "I understand your agitation" "Ah" "It's only the lungs" "Ah" "Breathe deeply" "Yes" "Breathe while you read. Don't stop reading" "Why?" "In order not to lose your breath" "I could lose it?" "You could lose it and no longer" "No longer breathe?" "Never again breathe" "That's what you told Franz?" "That's what I told my brother..." "And he breathed?" "He breathed while reading books... And he breathed while talking to me..." "You think we likewise breathe while reading and while breathing, I mean while talking…" "Franz did not breathe. Franz wheezed" "I'd like to talk to you" "I'm listening" "I know a man who searches for his pulse while reading" "Are you sure he is reading?" "No" "What is he doing?" "He is not reading and not talking" "He is not a man" "But I know he loves his sister" "He loves his sister, but does he love man?" "He loves to turn him into writing" "I'm going. Don't leave anything to chance" "I don't understand" "Stay close to the pulse and close to the book" "Yes" "Stay close to the man" "Yes" "Stay a bit longer" "Yes, but why?" "To understand him and turn him into writing" "Is there a difference?" I ask "No," she replies "I find you asocially beautiful" "You find me asocially beautiful" "Yes, beautiful and asocial" "I don't understand" "And yet your brother…" "My brother never explicates, he complicates, he implies" "Ah, and does not go as far as to apply what he explains, you mean" "I don't understand."

I raise my head from my book and my conversation with Franz's sister. Paul is staring at me. He looks at me the way he looked at my black tie the other day. The menace is real.

—I saw your lips move, form syllables. What did you want to tell me?

—It's a kind of defense.

—Against whom?

—Myself.

—Ah, you are afraid of yourself?

—Sometimes… I play at being afraid of myself.

—And at certain moments you are really afraid?

—Perhaps…

—What sort of defense do you have?

—Simply moving my lips.

—And your lips form syllables—real ones?

—Yes…

—So you talk.

—Mmmm…

—There are three possibilities: either you're talking to someone or you're talking to me or you're talking to yourself. Which is it?

—This is difficult to answer because the persons are superposed and cannot be named.

—You say that so that memory should no longer aid our recollection. It is an aid in talking to one another and in writing. The poem is the last surface of a given memory. It is the face of a die.

—The die is dead.

Long silence. The confrontation is dangerous. The silence becomes heavy. He breaks it:

—Am I to understand *dieu* or *dé,* god or die?

—*Dé.* The die is dead.

—Now I understand your black tie better. Why is the die dead?

—Because our lips divulge the sides of a game where dice have nothing to gamble for, neither god nor master.

—You like to play with words as fingers do with dice. You believe a tactile mass can imprint and throw the face of the die you choose in your head… There is no transparency. Things, words have a thickness, a density, also a shadow. Two words can cast the same shadow, right, over the verb that disappears for the reader, but does not disappear for the poem.

—The very disappearance of the verb allows the poem to exist.

—As the non-appearance of a character can sustain a narrative…

—Or the subject of the novel.

—The disappearance of the verb is precisely the subject.

—The disappearance imprints its history on the subject. I have wondered why. Why did the verb stay captive in our language, held back by it?

It is starting to rain outside. Outside, it rains, it is starting to rain, and I look at the rain. I look at Paul in front of the rain, against the light: tense, cutting, and without verb.

—Man is without verb. He is perhaps born of the verb, but he loses it. Life makes him lose it.

—Life furnishes the occasion of losing it…

—To gambling, you mean…

—To dice.

—To the invisible dice that roll in our steps. Seductive idea. I'm going to turn on the light. You can't see any more. Would you like to stay and have dinner with me? We'll go to La Chope. I've never asked you if you like coming as far as the Contrescarpe.

—The village is engaging.

—The passer-by is still a passer-by. A crowd is less anonymous than a passer-by.

—Mmmm…

—Let this translation be. We'll look at it next time.

How to speak of Paul Celan's—really unforeseeable—death and Gisèle's tears; that is, of this undercurrent of conversation that stays with me and surfaces, sometimes unflaggingly, in commentaries or subtitles of which I do not see either the need or the method. And Paul and Gisèle are each, separately, unflagging. Paul and the word during the day. Gisèle and the other word in the evening. Unflagging and mysterious moment, unflagging mystery. A path comes to connect Rue d'Ulm and Rue de Longchamp. An unflagging bridge unfolds with, sometimes, the feel of a flying-folding-talking carpet. The sun shines black. I climb the five flights and in my head rise above the paulownias, from which point I discover a web of streets and pain. I have a thought for the tired man: "Paul, between his four walls, chases after the sky."

[...]

We walk up Rue Soufflot. Beautiful sun, the mass of leaves of the Luxembourg behind us. Today, the first man walks on the moon. Paul smiles. Joyful and somber. His joy can darken very quickly. Hands behind his back, he walks along the sidewalk of Rue Soufflot with unusual energy: I have the impression that he is climbing rather than walking, hoisting himself up rather than just moving forward. We sit down on a terrace:

—The first man on the moon! There always has to be a first man. A discovery presupposes a first man and some surprises.

—Ah.

—In discovering other worlds, man will learn that all stars are empty and that he is alone. I say he is unique. I say he is alone.

—With a lot of sky around him.

—Too much sky. And a sky without color.

—Without angels.

—Angels are in the mind and in books. And only man prints those.

—You imagine the universe made of empty closets turned into satellites by other empty closets.

—Empty closets, but occupied by a few clothes hangers swinging ceaselessly...

—Yes... hangers and trembling...

He smiles.

—And on which path have you encountered them?

—The closets or the hangers?

—No! The angels.

—I found them in Rilke, after having found them in my childhood, really, literally in my childhood garden. I'd been adopted by houses whose garden was separated from mine only by a hedge with holes from my frequent climbing through.

The neighbors were professional photographers. I was not only "the child next door," but an occasional walk-on. Luther and Hortense—the photographers—had turned an old greenhouse into a studio with several painted backdrops that invariably illustrated a marriage scene, a birth scene, or a scene with miners. To give more poignancy to the birth scene, Luther and Hortense called on me. I went through garden and hedge, climbed the stairs and put on angel wings that Hortense had sewn onto suspenders. I had to lean over the cradle of the newborn, one hand holding a swallow...

—Ah, said Paul, it must already have been ruminating... But I can imagine you as an occasional silent angel. For angels do not talk in photographs. They only talk in books.

—Mmmm... The décor of birth never changed: the same cradle, the same angel, the same wooden swallow. Only the newborn was not part of the studio...

—It had to be imported...

—Yes... and it was hell... there's much to be said about the screams of newborns and photography. Hortense had imagined using a universal doll, silent and malleable, but the mere idea scandalized the photographer and the families.

—Why was it hell?

—Because the angel, the presence of the angel at the cradle was to soothe, which the newborn resisted. The more insistent the angelic presence the more impatient the newborn. And the sessions were endless.

—You did this often?

—Once a week: Hortense did newborns on Thursdays. But there were emergencies.

—Paul becomes thoughtful:

—You talk to me of Hortense and the other day you talked of *hortensias*, hydrangeas. I was connecting them.

—As you one day connected Paula, Paul and paulownia.

—Yes. We're hatched in such nestings.

Paul Celan orders two more glasses of red wine.

Blue cold around the hamlet. I turn in circles. I walk and turn. Blue cold. Nails blue with cold. Rue Sainte-Geneviève is deserted. The Place de la Contrescarpe is deserted. Rue Descartes, Rue d'Ulm, Rue d'Ulm.

Rue d'Ulm is deserted. The École Normale is deserted. The clock. Echoes. The corridor deserted. The door almond green. I knock. Sound of a chair. A body gets up, moves, comes near. He opens. He smiles.
—I'm happy to see you. You brought your poems? I want to read them.

I show them to him. He is terribly tense while reading. He reads them standing in the middle of the room. He turns the pages savagely. Reads at top speed.
—I like them very much. I'd like to translate them.

I've often asked myself what reading space enters into speed. Or into slowness. Do we read deeply when we read slowly? Do we read superficially when we read fast? Do we read everything— absolutely everything—with speed and only with speed? Paul reads the five pages I give him very fast. Savagely. He looks at me.
—I'll translate them.

He smiles. The word—the verb conjugated in the future—is said slowly, sadly, chilling in its obscurity. I look down. Stark silence comes over us with a dark caress that lets the verb continue to ring in the future, with the pleasure and pain of silence. We go out. We walk.

—You protect yourself less against your violence. You write it.

—Mmmm…

—A walk is like a conversation: it puts distance between oneself and the other, a close distance, a distance made of a closeness that transforms the landscape of the soul into a murmur, a noising abroad.

—Mmmm…

—Noising abroad is most difficult.

—Yes, how to melt a sentence against the palate?

—The word must melt or crack, or perhaps crackle?

—There is thunder in…

—…this study of technique. There is thunder.

—Mmmm…

—Wouldn't you like to walk over to our chestnut trees?

—If you like.

Fall 1989. Rue Montorgueil. We meet again. With much emotion. The Mercure de France is reprinting my— enlarged—translations of Paul Celan under the title *Strette et Autres Poèmes*. Gisèle confirms her agreement. I find her apartment unchanged. I rush to the bookshelf. It is there with all the books. In Paul's arrangement. I don't need to search long for *Les Epaves* of Charles Baudelaire. The copy bought for 1 franc on the quais has been in its same place for twenty-five years. In spite of life and visitors. In spite of moving. She wants to put things under seal. Silence them. Almost.

—Paul costs me a lot… she says to me.

—Is there a debt on your side?

—You know. Try to understand. Every month I devote one week to correspondence about Paul. I sit at my table. For six days I write letters from morning to night without lifting my head. I write thirty on the average, and they are difficult.

I bring her a copy of the book to come out in May 1990, that is twenty years after Paul's death, with a bouquet of roses and wild-flowers that she loves. We have lunch. She seems elsewhere. Suddenly we start talking as in the old days. The exchange is passionate and the conversation goes on and on.
—There is no dessert…
—Mmmm…
She makes coffee. Gentle moves and silences. Almost evening. I get up. We kiss goodbye. There is the departure, the door to be gotten through. She smiles at me. Solemn:
—Some day, write the word "heart" for me. In my memory.

A last look from her among the trees full of birds on the Place des Deux-Ecus. She is sitting at a café terrace. Intense look and yellow light. An appeal? She is not alone. A few weeks later, Gisèle dies.

The day after her death I telephone Rue Montorgueil early in the morning. I recognize the voice that answers: it is Mercedes, the "cleaning woman" whom I've so often made laugh.
—Is Gisèle there?
—She is here, Monsieur Jean.
—In the bedroom?
—In the bedroom, Monsieur Jean.
—Is she at peace?
—She is at peace…

A few minutes later I take a plane. I go far away and for long. I am starting ten days of reportage. I cannot go to Gisèle's funeral.

One morning Edith and I sit at the table in the sunny kitchen. She makes a request with her large black eyes. I know her extreme economy of gesture. Always. Today she is talking, she whom I'd known stubbornly silent. At that time she'd cough rather than speak:

—I understand your silence.

—…

—You are not writing any more, right…

—…

—You are writing, right…

—…

—You are writing and not telling…

—…

—You are writing a great novel…

—…

—You are writing? Why don't you admit you are writing…

—Mmmm…

—You are writing. And it will be posthumous…

—…

—Your heart hurts me. Your silence hurts me.

—…

—So what are you writing?

—Mmmm…

—Tell me… You made love to her? I wonder if… I just read page 274. Did you read it also? It is flabbergasting. In many respects.

—…

—I'll make some wild rice? You want some?

—…

—Your friends are not happy with you. In fact, nobody is really pleased with you.

— …

—Those I see and those in heaven. They all tell me they are sad. Very.

—I hear them.

—Ah. They talk to you?
—I answer their patience.
—Ah.
—I know their limits. They are benevolent.
—Ah. The wild rice, I'll make some. But do you want it?
—...

I have lived near a donkey. Long ago I lived near a pink radiator. It could have been green or blue. My mother insisted on pink. The color of cheeks painted by Velasquez or of Francis Bacon's bidets. Today it comes back to haunt me. It's the object of my childhood and my nursery. In summer it is cold. In winter it is scorching. It sits under the big window that looks out on the garden and the park. It shares my readings. One evening I read:

Faust: Fair lady, let it not offend you/That arm and escort I would lend you.

Margarete: I'm neither lady, neither fair,/And home I can go without your care.

She disengages herself and flees.[21]

The obvious is a mystery. What happens when a man and a woman meet? When there is speech? I would like to go farther and tell a story. Describe a circle. Here goes:

It's true, I was formed by the Encyclopedia job I worked on seven days a week for eighteen years as much as by journalism. How does knowledge (reading all books and plotting out their mechanism in the form of concise articles) come to help research? How does research proceed in its field with the help of knowledge, i.e. of deduction? Among other things, when you have to check true and false while knowing that true is a construction of not false. Why am I writing this? I want to tell a complicated story and simplify it in the extreme:

It is 11 o'clock in the morning. Beautiful light. The first blue sky of spring. I am walking alone in Paris, near the Hôtel de Ville. Large sidewalk. A slight crowd. There appears the red face of a really strange woman. I stare at her. She's a ways off. She does not see me. She cannot see me. Her eyes are half-closed. We approach. She is very near, dressed in black skirt and vest with a white blouse from the thirties. We are a few steps from each other when I suddenly speak to her with incredible matter-of-factness:

—Madame, you are traveling with Marcel Broodthaers' suitcase.

—But... I'm his wife, Maria.

We both laugh. And don't separate. We spend two days walking and talking together. All of Marcel Broodthaers' life told in the streets and under the chestnut trees:

—There is a real problem with beauty, as if doubt always gnawed on it and covered everything. Beauty and dust are so close.

—There is the same problem with the true and the not-false.

—I cannot reply to that, but I'll tell you a story. Broodthaers is a very handsome man. He talks a lot and even when doubtful projects great mastery. At least that's how others see him. He has extraordinary presence. He has a terrifying face. And everything he says carries...

—He has an eagle's look on the photos I've seen.

—A terrifying look. Especially these last years. Yes, the man, the artist, the person are fascinating. For many, Broodthaers is beauty. One day he exhibits his first eggs and first mussels. You know the mussels and eggs?

—Yes, I see them.

—And everybody, all the women say to me: "How sad, how disappointing... for so handsome a man to show eggshells, mussels. Tell him to stop it… Mussels glued on casserole lids and frenchfries in cartons… that's not art."

Later, at her house, she lets me read all of Marcel Broodthaers' manuscripts. All his book projects. Admirable. Suddenly, she says forcefully:
—I want you to meet a friend of Marcel Broodthaers': Panamarenko. He is exhibiting a pedal-airplane in a hangar.
On the occasion of some fact-checking I find myself again in Antwerp. In my rental car I search for Panamarenko's neighborhood, Rue des Abeilles, and his house. I go in. He is supposed to be expecting me. I discover green plants, motors and stray separate pieces of pedal-airplanes. His mother is there. Silent.
—Coffee?
—Mmmm…
—The son he come.
—Mmmm…
—You, wait.

We had met in Tours, in Paris, in Antwerp. Long conversations among Brasilian parrots and airplanes powered by human energy. Detached pedals. Detached wheels. Detached Mother. Panamarenko arrives. We prepare the dossier of drawings and texts to appear in *fig*, No.1, the periodical that picks up, twenty years later, from *fragment*, where I had published two poems by Paul Celan.

Am I clear? Am I abstract? In a nutshell: Donkey + Pink radiator + Faust and Margarete + Suitcase + Pedal-airplane = Paul Celan. How?

Rue d'Ulm. Paul Celan. Back from Berlin:

—I took the plane. It's a strange experience and I can tell you that a poem is like take-off and landing. There is... isn't there... apprehension, anxiety... right... But there's above all the search for an approach, for writing according to the axis of ground-lights.

—Mmmm...

—The search for ground-lights is not enough... There's the axis to be followed and... forgotten. You must above all find lightness—buoyancy—the permanent defiance of gravity.

—Mmmm...

—I wrote this poem in the plane. Read it. And why not keep and translate it for our book with Mercure de France?

The waters in the Luxembourg resound in the golden air that lines the paths. We make our rounds, finally pass through the gate, and he points to the terrace of a café. He watches me watch a young woman in the sun as she opens a silver cigarette case. With perfectly controlled nervousness her left hand handles an object so perfect and elegant that it troubles me. The lighter flame lights up her face showing extreme concentration.

—This woman troubles you because she too can write—with smoke. With her smoke against ours.

—She must write and she smokes with her soul.

—She writes and smokes with two fingers.

Winter returns. The cold is oppressive and stings the breath. I look at the starry sky through a windowpane as if through a sister's shadow, and my childhood hut also comes back into memory with the winter. Perhaps the mystery is to look at the sister herself as a star inside oneself?

I watch and wait. For night. The bare branches of the trees rise and seem stairs floating up the black air. The cold gently invades the dark. I am not walking. I am not looking at the three paulownias of the Contrescarpe. I am not walking down Rue Mouffetard, I am not crossing the Place des Patriarches. I'm waiting. I'm waiting and I'm talking. Tomorrow I'll be waiting and talking. Tomorrow.

The next day I indeed go up Rue Mouffetard and pass the four paulownias of the Contrescarpe. Indeed, winter. The *Bain-Douches* on Rue des Patriarches. Winter, passion, the *Bain-Douches* on Patriarches. Two things in fact: the *Bain-Douches* on Patriarches and the Fountain of the Innocents. I wait and don't talk. What is the reason? The stars have vanished. The night and the windowpane against which I yesterday watched my sister's presence have vanished.

[…]

I look at the stars. The little boy stares at a photograph, and the child runs. The chestnut trees form a vault over the sleep-walker. From a drainpipe, a man invites to a voyage whose miles are the chambers of my ear. I am a cat, I am cloven.

I wonder if, by staring at a photograph, the little boy does not eliminate its cause. It's autumn, season of leaves, of spades and garden chairs. The child drags the yellow lawnchair across the grass: he is raking in his fashion. And the photo he stares at is the enlargement of a fall as rust-red as the walls of the garden where, with bricks, boards and branches, he has built a hut where he learns to murmur a different language. Among the leaves, the ribs of leaves, the crackling and moving branches, the bony shadow of the walnut tree, the warm shadow of the chestnut tree, the firs, the holly, the hazels, the elder, the weeping birch, the peach tree. The autumnal landscape is the death of others. With big eyes I look at the blackbird. Vague shouts, and among the farther bushes moves a "maid" whose tough sex I'll come to know. She is sweeping without underpants. The broom is a holy instrument, and the dust too is holy. I fall asleep. I murmur and fall asleep under the linden. The ground at this spot of the garden remains humid. My body, a useless torment for it, does not sink in very deep.

I tell this to Paul who is attentive: garden, hut, murmur in hiding.

—You went from child and photography, right... to yourself...

—Ah.

—It is difficult to persevere in being. It... It often gives way and becomes I. Or perhaps It is I?... It is I. And...

—And I is a photo of Me.

—So I has photographic attributes.

—We should reread B. de S.

—Ah... who is that?

—Baruch de...

—Ah... Spinoza... You too have read...

—I know Statement and Attribute.

—Photographic attributes are more recent... And statement would insert an idea of God into the photographic attribute.

—God is photography. If photographer were an attribute of God...

—We would be Spinoza's Leicas.

—The attribute is Spinoza's Leica.

—When Spinoza searches for God in statement.

While telling this exuberant exchange, I recall a strange moment. Rue des Grands-Augustins, lunch time. I see in the distance André du Bouchet. In his left hand he holds an attaché-case and in his right, a can of tuna. He sees me and approaches. We say hello. André du Bouchet, while continuing to walk, puts the can of tuna on the edge of the attaché-case and shakes my hand. The two containers stay in balance: the tinned fish no heavier than the papers.

—A propos Leicas and photographic attributes, imagine Baruch polishing lenses and photographing God.
—Photographing God is not stating him.
—Yes, but Baruch polishes, hence...
—Polishing supposes...
—Using words without statement.
—Like a black sky... without stars.
—Statement is perhaps stellar, yes... like dice.
—Dice are gambled in our night. They gamble our night.
—And all the statements... without words.
—Like the sides with the numbers.
—Yes... like the sides with the numbers. Limited to six.
—Then we get to the decimal powers. God is the first.
—God is in the lens, in the magnifying glass, but not in Spinoza.
—That's why Baruch keeps polishing the divine image, which keeps escaping him in the statement. It is only in the statement that the image is a bit more real, not in the polishing.
—Mmmm...
—What if the stars were lenses polished by celestial hands?
—Mmmm...

Today the paulownias seem distant, behind ordinary lenses. Today the world is a lens, statements come with autumn that blurs them, and rakes polish God veiled in vague forms. Rakes. Rakes polish God, polish a vague mourning in which God veils an image of woman, into which a child's stammer vanishes.

—Don't forget that you have learned to read, but the world is always one library ahead.

—So the reader is always one library behind the world.

—And the world is nothing compared to what it could be once written.

—What would it be if not written.

—It could be spoken… stared at, *dé-vi-sa-gé*…

—It could be spoken language…

—Without books.

—And without readers.

—There would be only actors and rakes.

—And lenses to polish.

While telling this exuberant exchange, I do not want to pass over a strange encounter.

I am walking through the streets of a Southern city. Slowly. In dense shade. A young woman is following me. My shoulders get heavy. I turn around, she looks at me. She comes closer, and I owe it to myself to speak to her. She is very pale, beautiful, very mysterious. We have green tea with a puzzling ceremony. She pours very little water on the tea and lets the bottom of the cup infuse, waiting. She opens her purse, takes out a yellow box containing a small golden rake with which she mixes this small amount of tea and rakes it in circles. We spend the afternoon together. She opens her legs and notebooks and explains that her life is phonetic writing learned in Northern India among monkeys with whom she lived for a year. She says: "Before we part, I want to comb with my golden rake, in front of you watching, the hair on my vulva, my pubic triangle, the model of democracy. Before we part I shall give it to you."

I ask her to put off her departure or, more precisely, delay her vanishing. She listens. "I shall remain in vanishing."

That summer, like the previous ones, I have rented two rooms. I occupy the first. I do not occupy the second: I leave it empty. The two rooms are almost neighbors, separated by a square with a monument to the dead that makes one smile. I propose she should stay in the second room. She says: "Yes." The next afternoon I find her in her room. She has set up her red tent at the bottom of the bed and is there, naked, waiting: "Look, I rake my triangle, the model of democracy."

One day Karol has disappeared. With her rake. The story of this encounter is too long, too dense. I must not write it.

The chestnut trees again. The shade of the chestnut trees again. Their dome does not muffle the sounds before us. We walk under it. We walk with it. We carry it with us. Paul Celan:

—I like to look at a straw in someone's Coca-Cola bottle.
—Ah.
—But imagine a straw in eternity!
—In eternity?
—Yes. How insert eternity into a straw and a bubble into eternity.
—Perhaps if it were an angel of straw...

Other chestnut trees, later. And shade, later. Without straw. The evenings are humid, pink and humid. Again we are walking. He probes me. His look seems to come in lamellae. I hear him mutter. The silence intensifies. I don't know his reproach. I don't know his fear. We avoid each other: beginning of an ethics. He knows we should avoid each other. Life cannot pass into words. Look at the trees: he looks at them, and the torment of branches is a cartography suspended above us. He looks at me sideways and avoids me. October.

This is like night, and ink is setting, setting down the trees and their branches, whose domes larger than us walkers underneath plunge us into night and ink. We are the paper, things write us and set us down.

—All the chestnut trees are on the same meridian, he says.

—And all eternity is in the same straw.

—Ah yes! We walk on a rope, sipping eternity.

By the wayside (I'm avoiding the word a), the city is no longer there. I hear murmurs, feel commotion in our legs. By the wayside. As if the city were reduced to a ruined hut. Paul Celan:

—All people need is a perch. Not to perch on, because they have not talked in a long time, but to put a parrot on and be silent forever.

—Ah.

—This way they hear a parrot talk to them, and I didn't say that they learn to talk. For entire days they'll have a phrase in their ear. The buzz of a syllabic world.

—What is the language of the parrot?

—The rot of incest.

—Can it find its vocabulary in a parrot?

—A parrot can.

—And incest can too?

—Incest can find all moans, even those of a parrot.

—Incest can find all moans? You mean there is thinking in a parrot's moans? But what would he have lost?

—The parrot has lost and ruined man. And still talks to him in his own language as if man were still alive.

—And there is emptiness.

—Emptiness of emptiness.

—Because the parrot talks for nothing... for no-one.

—For man without his perch.

The world too is no longer there by the wayside. We are outlined against the windows lighting up. Slight sounds from the branches.

—Life becomes empty of father and mother and of us… A very ancient whirlwind that heats paradise.

—Our temperature is that of paradise?

—Our temperature is a mystery, how can it reproduce us in a book?

He begins to talk to himself.

—The distant ones do not have distant sorrows. They have our temperature and the unknown and the dark.

—Except for the sun.

—The sun has no distant sorrow: it shows gold.

—And purity in a gutter.

—Yes.

Silence in the courtyard of his building in Rue Tournefort where, much later, a friend will drop a deck of cards from the second floor. Bony silence, full of tiny cracklings. I imagine Paul calling "Eric."

The silence is rent. His cry. Yells. Windows light up. Night. The neighbors. Police. The station. Paul in tears. His hand over his forehead. Calcified logic. "This man hears voices." "Yes, he hears voices and talks to them." The neighbors also talk. Testify. Gossip.

A few years later. After Paul's death. Edith is with me. Beautiful, black "Spanish" look, in boots. It is snowing, and she is searching for an apartment for us both. She has been checking the ads for weeks.

She has finally found a studio at the Contrescarpe... Rue Tournefort.

"Rue Tournefort?" "Yes, Rue Tournefort. Why?" "Why? No reason."

Obviously Edith knows nothing about Rue d'Ulm, the Contrescarpe, Rue Tournefort and Paul. A fair reversal. We go to Rue Tournefort. I push the gate and discover finally the incredible courtyard where our steps echo with downright "incestuous" violence. I discover the hallways with their pipes, wires, plumbing. I imagine Paul coming home, walking along these cables. We were happy, insouciant, lighthearted. Many images come back to me. Sitting on the sofa, the most silent, somber, and today most talkative: Pascal Quignard and Alain Veinstein. CRJ and Pierre Rottenberg praise Clint Eastwood (in 1973). One Saturday evening, Edith on the phone under the framed portrait of Freud. Pierre Rottenberg shuts up the friends (CRJ, Alain Veinstein, Pascal Quignard): "Sh. Edith is calling Freud!" These events enter a space that I keep secret for being unable to talk of it. Nobody knows. What? I wait to be able to formulate the question: "What does being touched by fire allow you to write? Or: "What is the meaning of lightning before man, before the Gods?"

I am thinking this vaguely and without words in the studio of Rue Tournefort, leaning out the window and looking down on the courtyard. Edith, her big black frightened eyes that I stare at and stare at her black eyes. How do we look at lightning? Yes, how? For a long time. With a look that imprints the lightning, for a long time. And beyond.

NOTES:

1 From "Hörreste, Sehreste," a poem about the "re-education" in the psychiatric clinic. In *Lichtzwang* (1970, published posthumously).

2 *Décimale blanche* is Jean Daive's first book of poetry (Mercure de France, 1967).

3 In *Lichtzwang*.

4 Klaus Demus: Austrian poet.

5 In 1953, Claire Goll accused Paul Celan of having plagiarized poems by her late husband, Yvan Goll. The charge was groundless.

6 *L'Ephémère*: literary magazine edited by the poet André du Bouchet.

7 Daniel Cohn-Bendit: leader of the student protests during May 1968 in France.

8 *énoncé*: usually rendered as statement. Jean Daive defines: "An *énoncé* is a group of words or formulas that constitute a unity. I say: the *énoncé* of a law or the *énoncé* of a theorem or the *énoncé* of a proposition. The *énoncé* is a world apart. It has its strangeness, but always its logic because it starts from one point and arrives at another point by foreseeable steps."

9 Brain-cry: *Le cri-cerveau* is the title of Jean Daive's second book of poems (1977).

10 "Einmal,/da hörte ich ihn," in *Atemwende* (1967).

11 CRJ: Claude Royet-Journoud.

12 "Du liegst im grossen Gelausche," in *Schneepart* (1971), on the murder of Rosa Luxemburg & Karl Liebknecht. "Sieve and sow": Liebknecht was riddled with bullets like a sieve; Luxemburg's body was thrown into the Landwehrkanal and jeered at by the murderers: "The old sow is swimming."

13 *Der Meridian*: speech Celan gave on the occasion of receiving the Georg-Büchner-Preis (1960).

14 "Und mit dem Buch aus Tarussa," in *Die Niemandsrose* (1963).

15 Group 47: "*Gruppe 47*," a German literary group founded in 1947 (by Hans Richter et al.) to encourage young authors in post-war Germany. The meetings consisted of authors reading from manuscripts, followed by criticism from established literary critics. Prizes were awarded at each meeting. The year Celan was invited, 1953, Ingeborg Bachmann received the prize. The group was disbanded in 1977.

16 "L'épine n'est pas ce que vous croyez, elle n'est pas cette colline." A play on épine, thorn, thornbush and "*épine dorsale*," spine, backbone, also used for the crest of a hill.

17 Allusion to *Le cornet à dés [The Dice-Cup]*, a book of prose poems by Max Jacob, and, on the next page, to Mallarmé's *Un coup de dés... [A Throw of Dice...]*.

18 Montesquieu held that we are all prisoners and must therefore try to find a file wrapped in wet cloth to quietly saw through the bars millimeter by millimeter.

19 The quotations from Spinoza are given in the translation of A.Wolf, *The Correspondence of Spinoza*, New York, 1927.

20 "the Littré": *The Dictionnaire de la langue française* of Emile Littré is the French equivalent of the *Oxford English Dictionary*.

21 Quoted in the translation of Bayard Taylor.

[...]: all ellipses are the author's.

Jean Daive, Place de la Contrescarpe, 2020

Author of over fifteen collections of poetry and seven volumes of fiction, JEAN DAIVE has been an important voice in French letters for over 35 years. His first book of poetry, *Décimale blanche,* published in 1967, received much attention; his subsequent volumes have often been ongoing, serial volumes—*Narration d'équilibre, Trilogie du Temps, La Condition d'infini*—each exploring a specific concept and/or formal question across three or more volumes. Daive's work has received extensive critical attention, both in full-length volumes and numerous articles. Also a translator, he has published translations of the poetry of Paul Celan, Robert Creeley, Norma Cole, and others. Daive has also exerted great influence: during his decades of work in radio, as a producer at France Culture; as president of the Centre International de Poésie à Marseille (CiPM); and as the founder and editor of four successive poetry journals: *Fragment* in 1969, *fig.* in 1989, *Fin* in 1999, and *K.O.S.H.K.O.N.O.N.G.* in 2013. He lives and works in Paris.

Poet, translator, and editor ROSMARIE WALDROP has been a forceful presence in American and international poetry for over forty years. Born in Germany in 1935, Waldrop studied literature and musicology before immigrating to the United States in the late 1950s. She received a Ph.D. from the University of Michigan in 1966. While at the University of Michigan, Waldrop married poet and translator Keith Waldrop. She has lived in Providence, Rhode Island, since 1968 and she has taught at Wesleyan University, Tufts, and Brown. She has become the leading English translator of Edmond Jabès's writing, translating over a dozen volumes of his work. In 1993 she was awarded the Harold Morton Landon Translation Award for her translation of Jabès's *The Book of Margins,* and was named "Chevalier des Arts et des Lettres" by the French government. Waldrop has authored over 20 books of her own writing, including poetry, fiction, and essays. In 2006 she was elected to the American Academy of Arts and Sciences.

ROBERT KAUFMAN is an associate professor of Comparative Literature at the University of California, Berkeley, where he also teaches in, and is past co-director of, the interdisciplinary Program in Critical Theory. Kaufman is the author of *Negative Romanticism: Adornian Aesthetics in Keats, Shelley, and Modern Poetry* (forthcoming from Cornell University Press in 2021), and is at work on two related books, *Why Poetry Should Matter—to the Left: Frankfurt Constellations of Democracy* and *Modernism after Postmodernism? Robert Duncan and the Future-Present of American Poetry.* His essays on modern poetry, aesthetics, and critical theory have been published in numerous journals and edited volumes.

PHILIP GERARD received his Ph.D. in Comparative Literature and Critical Theory from the University of California, Berkeley in 2019; he is currently a research fellow at the Centre interdisciplinaire d'étude des littératures at the University of Lausanne, Switzerland. Gerard's article "Pound Notes in German Markets: Paul Celan, Usury, and the Postwar Currency of Ezra Pound" appeared in the January 2020 issue of *Modernism/modernity*, and he is completing a book manuscript on poetic transmission and ruptured history with the provisional title *Speaking After: Ezra Pound, Paul Celan, and the Modernist Task of the Translation.*

Under the Dome, Rosmaire Waldrop's translation of Jean Daive's book *Sous la Coupole* (P.O.L., 1996), was originally published in 2009 by Burning Deck, the small press she and her husband Keith Waldrop ran for some 56 years. Founded in 1961 in Ann Arbor, Michigan, the press accompanied the Waldrops to Durham, Connecticut, in 1964 and then to Providence, Rhode Island, in 1968. There Burning Deck would remain—a vital resource for American and British poetry as well as translations of contemporary French and German writing—until it ceased publishing in 2017. Much of this history is recounted in the excellent dossier on Rosmarie and Keith Waldrop, *Keeping/ the window open: Interviews, statements, alarms, excursions* (Wave Books, 2019), edited by Ben Lerner.